CAMBRIDGE LIBRARY COLLECTION

Books of enduring scholarly value

Latin American Studies

This series focuses on colonial Latin America and the Caribbean. It includes historical and statistical reference works from the eighteenth and nineteenth centuries, reports describing scientific, archaeological and ethnological expeditions, and editions of accounts from the earliest period of European settlement.

A Description of Patagonia, and the Adjoining Parts of South America

Thomas Falkner (1707–84), one-time pupil of both Richard Mead and Isaac Newton, was an English Jesuit missionary who lived for nearly forty years in South America until 1767, when he returned to England following the Jesuits' expulsion from Córdoba. Originally published in 1774 in the hope that it 'might be of some public utility, and might also afford some amusement to the curious', this is a first-hand description of Patagonia, believed to have been consulted by Charles Darwin on board the *Beagle*. Illustrated with a map drawn from the author's knowledge and experience, it is an account of the dramatic physical geography of the area as well as the customs, beliefs and language of its inhabitants. Falkner's narrative ranges from a discussion of the virtues of American tea (in certain particulars 'far excelling the tea of China') to a detailed depiction of the role of wizards and rituals involving demons.

T0364267

Cambridge University Press has long been a pioneer in the reissuing of out-of-print titles from its own backlist, producing digital reprints of books that are still sought after by scholars and students but could not be reprinted economically using traditional technology. The Cambridge Library Collection extends this activity to a wider range of books which are still of importance to researchers and professionals, either for the source material they contain, or as landmarks in the history of their academic discipline.

Drawing from the world-renowned collections in the Cambridge University Library and other partner libraries, and guided by the advice of experts in each subject area, Cambridge University Press is using state-of-the-art scanning machines in its own Printing House to capture the content of each book selected for inclusion. The files are processed to give a consistently clear, crisp image, and the books finished to the high quality standard for which the Press is recognised around the world. The latest print-on-demand technology ensures that the books will remain available indefinitely, and that orders for single or multiple copies can quickly be supplied.

The Cambridge Library Collection brings back to life books of enduring scholarly value (including out-of-copyright works originally issued by other publishers) across a wide range of disciplines in the humanities and social sciences and in science and technology.

A Description of Patagonia, and the Adjoining Parts of South America

THOMAS FALKNER

CAMBRIDGE UNIVERSITY PRESS

Cambridge, New York, Melbourne, Madrid, Cape Town,
Singapore, São Paolo, Delhi, Mexico City

Published in the United States of America by Cambridge University Press, New York

www.cambridge.org
Information on this title: www.cambridge.org/9781108060547

© in this compilation Cambridge University Press 2013

This edition first published 1774
This digitally printed version 2013

ISBN 978-1-108-06054-7 Paperback

A
DESCRIPTION
OF
PATAGONIA,

AND THE

Adjoining Parts of SOUTH AMERICA:

CONTAINING AN

Account of the Soil, Produce. Animals, Vales, Mountains, Rivers, Lakes, &c. of thofe Countries;

THE

Religion, Government, Policy, Cuftoms, Drefs, Arms, and Language of the INDIAN Inhabitants;

AND SOME

Particulars relating to FALKLAND's ISLANDS.

By THOMAS FALKNER,
Who refided near Forty Years in thofe PARTS.

ILLUSTRATED WITH
A New Map of the Southern Parts of AMERICA,
Engraved by Mr. KITCHIN, HYDROGRAPHER to His MAJESTY.

HEREFORD:
Printed by C. PUGH; and fold by T. LEWIS, Ruffell-Street, Covent-Garden, London.

M.DCC.LXXIV.

ADVERTISEMENT.

OUR knowledge of the Countries and Inhabitants of the Southern Hemifphere has been of late confiderably enlarged, and it is hoped that the prefent publication may prove no unacceptable addition to what has been written on that fubject. It is needlefs to point out to the curious reader the feveral circumftances of agreement or difagreement, in manners and language, between the nations here defcribed and others we have had accounts of. But it may be proper to take notice, that a great difference will be found between M. Bougainville and our Author, with regard to Falkland's Iflands; which muft be left to the judgment of the public.

When the Preface was printed off, it was not intended that the Author's name fhould have been mentioned; but a certain unexpected event has removed all fcruples on that head.

CONTENTS.

PREFACE.

INTRODUCTION.

Of the most southern part of America, described in the map.

CHAPTER I.

Of the soil and produce of the most southern part of America.

* This city, which is north of Cordova, is not within the limits of the map.

CHAP-

CHAPTER II.

Defcription of the Indian country, with its vales, mountains, rivers, &c.---Great River La Plata, with its branches, fifh, and ports.

CHAPTER III.

Continuation of the defcription of the Indian country, with its vales, mountains, rivers, &c.---Tierra del Fuego.---Falkland's Iflands.

CHAPTER IV.

An account of the inhabitants of the moft fouthern part of America, defcribed in the map.

CHAPTER V.

The religion, government, policy, and cuftoms, of the Moluches and Puelches.

CHAPTER VI.

An account of the language of the inhabitants of thefe countries.

P R E F A C E.

THE eftablifhment of an Englifh colony in Falkland's Iflands is faid to be in confequence of an opinion of the late Lord Anfon, who thought that a fettlement, and the fecuring a good harbour for Englifh fhips, in the fouthern feas of America, was a proper meafure for extending the commerce and marine empire of Great Britain. This confideration induced me to imagine, that any information concerning the geography, inhabitants, and other particulars, of the moft fouthern part of the American continent, might be of fome public utility, and might alfo afford fome amufement to the curious. Wherefore, becoming acquainted with a perfon who had refided near forty years in South America, and had been employed in furveying and making charts of the country, I obtained the favour of him to make a map, according to what he had himfelf obferved, and what he had difcovered from the relation of others; to which he added a defcription of the country, and of the Indian inhabitants. He has alfo mentioned fuch particulars of the productions of the country as may be articles of commerce, or were of fervice in his medical profeffion. Some alteration has been made in the language and order of what he had

B

wrote;

wrote; but nothing has been added to the narrative of the old traveller.

Another reason for this publication is, that whenever a thorough reconciliation takes place between the courts of London and Madrid, it is probable that English merchants may be again permitted to carry on the slave trade, and perhaps some other branches of commerce in the River of Plate.

The Spaniards having no settlements on the coasts of Africa, where the slaves are bought, have made Assiento contracts; that is, let as a farm, to merchants of other nations, a contract for supplying Spanish America with African slaves.

The English South Sea Company had an exclusive grant of such a contract from the making of the peace of Utrecht until the war broke out with Spain in the year 1739; and the Company had a factory at Buenos-Ayres, from whence the slave trade was carried on much more advantageously, not only with the great provinces of Buenos-Ayres, Paraguay, and Tucuman, but likewise with the kingdoms of Peru and Chili, than it was by Portobello and Panama. The voyage is much shorter; the climate healthier; and provisions better, and in greater plenty; horses and land-carriage are so cheap, that European goods may be sent from Buenos-Ayres to Potosi, and other parts of Peru, at a less expence, and with less hazard, than to Portobello, carried over the isthmus, and re-shipped at Panama for the ports of Peru and Chili. Buenos-Ayres, and the harbours of the River of La Plata, are not only of great importance to the Spaniards in the course of trade, but their empire in South America in great measure depends on their being in possession of those harbours; for their ships going round Cape Horn to Chili and Peru, must in that

long

long voyage be supplied with provisions in the River of Plate, or depend upon the Portuguese, and put into some port of the Brazils.

As it is probable that English ships may one day enter the River of Plate, either as friends or enemies, the harbours in that river are described, and an account is given of the fish that are there taken. A plan of the river would likewise have been given, but that there is one already published in Charlevoix's History of Paraguay, in which the soundings were set down with great accuracy; but alterations frequently happen in the sand banks of that river. Since the French and Spanish Monarchs have entered into their family compact, French trading vessels are often seen in the River of Plate, and other Spanish American harbours, and a company of French merchants are said to have obtained a grant of the Assiento contract. The English may again be the favoured nation in the Spanish trade, as they were formerly: for of all the commercial treaties, which the court of Spain had agreed to with foreign nations, there were none so favourable as that of 1676 with the English, as Sir William Godolphin, the minister employed in making that treaty, asserts in a letter to Lord Arlington.

In order to shew that there are grounds for the conjecture, that, at some future period of time, the English may be considered as the most useful and desirable allies of the Spaniards, and on whom they may rely with the greatest safety, it will be necessary for me to exceed the bounds of an introductory discourse; but the subject is interesting, and what I offer may give occasion to its being treated in a more ample and better manner.

If the mutual wants, and common interests, of the subjects of Great Britain and of Spain, are considered in all

their

their different relations to each other, and to other powers, it will appear, that there are no two nations in the world, to whom a perpetual alliance would bring greater and more permanent advantages. The Spaniards are fo convinced of the truth of this affertion, that it has long been a proverbial faying among them, *Peace with England and War with all the World*; and Sir William Temple obferves, that the Spaniards, in his time, *placed their hope in England, where their inclination carries them as well as their intereft.* When the Kings of Spain were more powerful than at prefent, and when they were Sovereigns of all, or of a confiderable part of the Netherlands, there might, on the part of the Englifh, be fome objections to a clofe and lafting union with the Spaniards. The vicinity of the Flemifh harbours, and the manufactures and courfe of trade of the Englifh and Flemifh merchants being nearly the fame, were caufes of jealoufy and contention, befides many other political views that no longer exift, fince the Kings of Spain have been deprived of all the Seventeen Provinces of the Low Countries. A miftaken zeal for religion has fometimes prevented advantageous alliances; but that is daily becoming lefs inclined to violent meafures, and lefs connected with the general policy of the ftate.

The many arguments for toleration, publifhed in this and towards the latter end of the laft century, though they have not brought about all the good effects that may hereafter be expected from the moft beneficent principles fupported by the cleareft reafoning, yet they have at leaft fo far had their influence in the councils of Chriftian Princes, that an union in religion feems no longer a motive in forming their treaties, nor will a difference in divine

worfhip

worſhip be the cauſe of diſcord between nations whoſe political and commercial intereſts coincide.

Trade is an objeƈt, to which the powers of Europe give great attention, and which ought to be conſidered as a principal bond of union between the Engliſh and the Spaniards; becauſe the articles of commerce, that is, the overplus of the produce, of Spain and of the Spaniſh colonies, conſiſts of things that are particularly wanting in Great Britain, or are abſolutely neceſſary for carrying on the Britiſh manufaƈtures, in their preſent degree of perfeƈtion. The wine, oil, and fruits of Spain, cannot ſerve in barter for French manufaƈtures, as the French have thoſe commodities of their own growth; and they can be brought to no market in ſuch quantities, and ſo much to the advantage of the Spaniards, as to Great Britain and Ireland. This trade might be extended; as there are many excellent ſorts of wine, made in the interior parts of Spain, which might be exported, if the roads were opened, and ſome inland duties taken off. The Peruvian bark, and many other medicinal drugs, are brought to us only from Spain or Spaniſh America. The wool, ſilk, cotton, cork, indigo, cochineal, logwood, cocoa nut, and other articles, are ſent to England, as far as poſſible, in their firſt growth; ſo that the employment of the artificer, and the profit ariſing from his labour, center in this kingdom.

The Spaniards have hitherto taken more from England and her colonies than the amount of their exports, and the balance has been paid chiefly in ſilver; which ſupplies us with the current ſpecie and the wrought plate, and ſupports the trade of the Eaſt India Company.

It is difficult to gueſs how far the trade may be extended, to the benefit of both nations; for we muſt imagine that, in

C

ſuch

fuch a vaft country as Spanifh America, with fuch a variety of foils and climates, and in fome parts abounding with minerals of every kind, new veins of commerce will frequently be difcovered. The falt-petre, and the dried leaves of the tea plant, which are mentioned in this work, may one day be exchanged for Britifh manufactures, inftead of draining this kingdom of the filver, with which thofe commodities are now purchafed in Bengal and in China. The exports from hence to Spain are chiefly Britifh manufactures; of which there is fcarce any fpecies fabricated in England, Scotland, or Ireland, but what is proper for the Spanifh trade.

The prefent ftate of agriculture in Spain occafions the inhabitants to be fometimes in want of corn, which has been often fent from England, and with which, from hence forwards, they will probably be fupplied from the Englifh North American colonies. The Spanifh fhips could not be victualled without the provifions that are fent from thofe colonies and from Ireland. The Spaniards alfo take from the Englifh great quantities of falted and dried fifh; which contributes much to the fupport of thofe nurferies of feamen, the Newfoundland and Britifh fifheries.

The courfe of trade of each nation no where thwarts, or is carried on in oppofition to the trade of the other, if we except the contraband trade from Jamaica; which would ceafe, or be fuppreffed, as would likewife that of other nations, if the Englifh were favoured in the regular Spanifh commerce, and the cargoes fent from Europe, in the galleons, flota, and regifter fhips, were fold in Spanifh America confiderably cheaper than they are at prefent. This might eafily be done, without diminifhing the public revenue of the King of Spain, by altering the prefent complicated

cated and uncertain mode of taxation, and by abolifhing unneceffary formalities, tedious delays, and expenfive applications to the Spanifh minifters; which encumber the licenfed trade, and greatly enhance the price of the merchandize fold in America, and at the fame time diminifh the value of what is fent back from thence; which would be increafed by the quicknefs of the return, much to the advantage of the Creoles, and of the Spaniards themfelves.

Another caufe of contention was the right of cutting logwood on the coafts of the Bay of Honduras, which had long been oppofed by the Spanifh government, but which was given up to the Englifh by an article in the laft peace. And difcord may have been prevented by a farther conceffion, likewife obtained in the fame treaty; which was, the Spaniards relinquifhing all pretenfions to the fifhery on the banks of Newfoundland. The Bifcayners are thought to have been the firft mariners who went on that fifhery, and if the firft poffeffion gave any right, it was transferred by that article to the Englifh.

An attempt to explain minutely every branch of commerce would be tedious to the generality of readers; but, I believe, the more this fubject is examined, the more clearly it will appear, that the true commercial interefts of the two kingdoms every way agree, or are reconcileable to each other. And nearly the fame may be faid in regard to the territories belonging to each kingdom; becaufe there is no territory poffeffed by the one, that can, in good policy, be an object of ambition to the other: for, excepting the rock of Gibraltar, there is not a fpot of ground under the dominion of the King of Great Britain, that a patriot King of Spain ought to wifh for; and that fortrefs, and the Ifland of

Minorca,

Minorca, might be confidered, more as ftore-houfes for the Mediterranean trade, than as military ftations : or, if they have a hoftile appearance, that may be neceffary, to fecure refpect to the Britifh flag from the Barbary corfairs, and ought not to raife fufpicions of an unfriendly difpofition in the Englifh towards the Spanifh nation. The province of Eaft Florida, which was ceded alfo by the treaty of Paris, in exchange for the Havanna, was of little or no confequence to the Spaniards in time of peace; in cafe of a war with England, that fettlement might have been an annoyance to the Englifh colonies. But, as it adjoins on one fide to Georgia and Carolina, and on the other to Weft Florida, which the French relinquifhed by the fame treaty, it muft have been an eafy conqueft to the Englifh; wherefore the Spaniards, while they wifh for peace with England, cannot regret the lofs of a burthenfome, defencelefs territory.

The river Miffifippi is the moft proper boundary, and the moft likely to prevent all future contefts. The largenefs of the river, and the length of it's courfe, makes it appear, as if formed by nature to fet bounds to the vaft empires of Britifh and Spanifh America. The prefent extenfivenefs of the Englifh colonies will probably delay their defection from the mother country, becaufe it will hinder the eftablifhment of confiderable manufactures; for men will not be inclined to work at the loom or the anvil, for the merchant or wholefale manufacturer, if they can obtain portions of land to be allotted to them, which they may cultivate entirely for their own advantage. The fubjection of thofe colonies to the Sovereign of Great Britain is, in fome refpects, of as much importance to Old Spain, as it is to Old England: for when the Britifh Americans become

independant,

independant, it will probably induce the inhabitants of the great kingdoms in Spanish America to follow their example; which they will alfo be forced to do, by their communication with Europe being intercepted; for North America is better provided with timber, and all kinds of naval ftores, than any other country in the world. A great maritime power will be formed there, and the people will have that bold, enterprizing fpirit, with which free governments generally animate mankind. In fuch circumftances, the Spanish Creoles muft have their commerce with the North Ameri cans. No treafure could with fafety be brought to Spain; the galleons and flota could not often efcape the North American cruizers, particularly in the windward paffage, and the narrow channel between the Bahama iflands and the continent. It feems therefore a reafonable conjecture, that an abfolute independancy of the North American colonies on the government of Great Britain would, in it's confequences, bring about, in all other parts of America, the fame independancy on the other nations of Europe. Such a revolution would be fatal to all Europeans, as it would bring them back to the poverty of their anceftors, and leave in the imaginations of many of them the cravings of modern luxury.

The interefts of the Britifh and Spanifh nations continue united, both in thefe diftant views, which depend on future contingencies, and likewife in many of their immediate and prefent relations to the neighbouring ftates.

France is the power, of which both nations ought to be jealous; an ambitious enterprizing Monarch, like Lewis the XIVth, would be a moft dangerous neighbour to both kingdoms. The meafures purfued by Oliver Cromwell, and by fome of our Kings, which raifed France, and funk

D   the

the power of Spain, are now perceived to have been contrary to the true interefts of the Britifh monarchy. Befides their common danger, to be apprehended from France, the relative grandeur of England, and of Spain, depends on preferving the general balance of power between the ftates of Europe, and the particular balance that fubfifts among the Republics and Princes of Italy. The liberty of the Dutch, of the Swifs, and of the Hanfe Towns, and the remains of the conftitution of the German empire, feem to be objects of great confequence in the fcale of power, according to which the Britifh and Spanifh monarchies are to be confidered.

The harmony, and national union, eftablifhed between them, would be the fafeft barrier againft any ambitious defigns of the court of France; it would have an influence in fettling the trade of the Englifh in Portugal; it might tend to deprefs the infolence of the piratical ftates of Africa, whofe corfairs have often infefted the coafts of Spain; and it might be a kind of bafis, on which the liberty of Europe, that is, the independancy of the different powers, might fafely reft. For if thofe powers are convinced that the Englifh do not defire to make conquefts on the continent of Europe, nor the Spaniards to extend their dominion beyond the Pyrenean mountains, fuch a difinterefted fyftem will give weight to their joint negotiations, and gain the confidence of other nations.

The principal objection to the plan of a lafting alliance may arife from the wars between England and Spain, and the almoft continual hoftile difpofitions that have appeared, ever fince the Princes of the Bourbon family afcended the Spanifh throne. This objection makes it neceffary to explain in what manner thofe wars were brought on; which

was

was by a fyftem of policy, that was foreign and contrary to the true interefts of the Spanifh nation. The fubferviency of the Court of Madrid to the councils, or rather mandates, of the French, ceafed on the death of Lewis XIV, and the Spaniards began to return to a fenfe of their own importance, and their natural jealoufy of powerful and ambitious neighbours: but their Sovereign Philip V, either from falfe ideas of Chriftian perfection, or from weaknefs of body, or mind, gave up the reins of government into the hands of his fecond confort. She was daughter of the Duke of Parma, and, although married to the King of Spain, yet her mind continued all Italian. It is a principal point of Italian patriotifm, to deliver Italy from a foreign yoke, and particularly from the dominion of the Germans; and this the Queen was ambitious of accomplifhing. She had another inducement for undertaking a war in Italy, which perhaps influenced her ftill more powerfully, and this was the providing kingdoms, or independant fovereignties, for all her fons. Thus the ambition of the Italian Princefs, and the fondnefs of the mother, overcame the fenfe of duty of the Queen, who directed the government of a great nation; for the wars were carried on, and the young Princes have been fupported, at a great expence of blood and treafure, without a profpect of advantage to the people of Spain. And as natives might be lefs active and vigilant in projects that were detrimental to their country, the Queen appointed Alberoni, an Italian cardinal; Riperda, a Dutchman; and other foreigners, for her minifters.

The defigns of the Queen were contrary to the political views of the Englifh, and the fyftem of the great alliance formed by King William; but coincided with the intereft of France; not only becaufe, by thefe means, the court

of

of Spain became united with, and dependant on the French, for the accomplishment of those designs, but likewise, because the settlements on the Spanish Princes were to be made by driving the Austrians out of Italy. So by entering into the views of the Queen of Spain, the French gained a rich ally, and at the same time weakened a powerful rival.

On the death of Philip V, the thoughts of making conquests in Italy were at an end; for his son by his first Queen, Ferdinand VI, who succeeded him, loved the Spanish nation, seldom spoke any other language but the Spanish, and employed none but Spanish ministers. As King Ferdinand had no children, the Dowager Queen, whose sons were to succeed to him, had a strong party in the court; but neither her influence, nor all the French intrigues, could bring him into the war against England; though they might prevent that union with the English, to which a discerning and truly patriotic King of Spain will always be inclined.

Ferdinand VI dying without issue, the kingdom of Spain devolved to the Queen Dowager's eldest son, Don Carlos, then King of Naples. He was, by former transactions, already disposed to join in the French interests; but the ministry of Versailles proposed binding him in a still closer union with France, and, for this purpose, they are thought to have set before him the prospect of himself or his descendants succeeding to the French monarchy, on failure of male issue of the elder branch of the Bourbon family. The late Dauphin was then in a very infirm state of health, and his sons were represented by Dr. Tronchin, as it is said, and the French physicians, as persons of a weakly constitution, not likely to live, or to leave posterity.

rity. On this a Family Compact was agreed upon between the two Monarchs; by the fecret articles of which it is fuppofed to have been ftipulated, that the Spanifh branch of the Houfe of Bourbon fhould fucceed to the Crown of France, for want of male defcendants of Lewis XV. The name of Family Compact, given to the treaty, indicates fome regulations in regard to family fucceffions, and would be an improper title, if there were no other articles in the treaty, but thofe which have been announced to the public. The reafon of the articles which relate to the fucceffion being kept fecret is very obvious; becaufe they are a violation of the treaty of Utrecht; in which Philip V renounced, in the cleareft manner, for himfelf and his defcendants, all future claims and pretenfions to the kingdom of France. The French minifter, Mr. De Torcy, endeavoured to evade that abfolute renunciation, as may be feen in his letters to Lord Bolingbroke; but the Englifh miniftry infifted upon it; and indeed it was the moft important point that was obtained by all the fucceffes in Queen Anne's war, which was undertaken to prevent the dependancy of Spain on the Court of France; whereas the intent of both the fecret, and the avowed articles, of the Family Compact, is to eftablifh that dependancy.

That there are fecret articles, relating to the Bourbon Family, may be inferred, not only from the title of the treaty, but likewife from thofe articles that have been made public; becaufe the two Sovereigns declare no other motives in thofe public articles, but their mutual regard for each other, and for the honour of their family; motives, which can only relate to themfelves, and not to the commerce or mutual naturalization of their fubjects. For it would be too humiliating to mankind, and debafing the dignity of

E human

human nature, to fuppofe that no attention is to be given by Princes to the well-being of the people they govern, or that the lives and fortunes of millions are of no other confequence in the eftimation of their Sovereigns, than as they contribute to the grandeur of a Monarch, and the glory of a Royal Family: and I am willing to imagine, that fome thoughts concerning the happinefs of their fub-jects are expreffed in the fecret parts of the treaty.

The two Monarchs had an example of the inordinate defire of family greatnefs in their anceftor Lewis XIV; who, after the death of the laft King of Spain of the Houfe of Auftria, was advifed by his council to abide by the difpofitions made in the partition treaty, and which would have been much more advantageous to the French nation, than to have acquired for Lewis's grandfon, the Duke of Anjou, the whole fucceffion of the Spanifh monarchy, under the will of the then late departed King of Spain; but Lewis determined on what he thought more glorious for his family, though it involved Europe in a long and bloody war, which brought his own kingdom to the brink of ruin. This fentiment was fo prevalent in the mind of the French Monarch, that he alleged in a manner no other motive but his own glory, for the war againft Holland in 1672. And he was offended at one of his fubjects, who, in fome public harangue, fpoke to him about the interefts of France, and the well-being of the ftate; becaufe it was his will and pleafure, that Frenchmen fhould have no other political principles but an enthufiaftic zeal for the glory of their So-vereign. The Englifhman's love of his country, and loy-alty to his King, are founded on more rational principles, and more honourable to human nature. Thofe two duties are happily united, by our having a Sovereign, who has

no

no interests that are distinct from those of the British nation, and whose family connections engage him in no wars or treaties that are prejudicial to his subjects, but who considers the peace and happiness of all his people as the sole end and glory of his reign.

Preparations were made for the Family Compact, by the French King's giving up the pretensions of his son-in-law, Don Philip, and of his grandson, the present Duke of Parma, to the kingdoms of Naples and Sicily. The eventual succession to those kingdoms was settled on them by the treaty of Aix-la-Chapelle, upon the contingency of Don Carlos, the then King of Naples, becoming King of Spain; but the French consented, that the Spanish Monarch might deprive his own brother of that succession, and afterwards his nephew (whose mother was daughter to the present King of France), and settle the kingdoms of Naples and Sicily on his third son.

In order the more to cement the union proposed to be established by the Family Compact, and that the French Court might give farther proofs of sincerity to the King of Spain, the Duke of Orleans, who is next in succession to the crown if the Spanish branch is excluded, and the other Princes of the blood, were deprived of that share, or influence in the French government, to which, by their birth, and by the custom or constitution of the kingdom, they have been generally understood to be entitled. The lowering the dignity and importance of those Princes in the opinion of the people of France may be considered as a part of the system of the Family Compact; and perhaps for the same motives the parliaments, or great courts of judicature, have been dissolved, and the patriotic lawyers banished or imprisoned; as such persons may be thought

to

to be inclined to maintain the validity of Philip V's renunciation, and likewife the fpirit and intent of the Salic
Law, which means to exclude foreign Princes from inheriting the Crown of France.

The Spanifh Monarch has, in like manner, banifhed or
difgraced all thofe who were thought to difapprove of the
Family Compact, and French fpies are employed in
moft of the confiderable towns of Spain, to watch the
difaffected to this new projected union with France.
Thefe proceedings feem to refemble the conduct of
Auguftus, Anthony, and Lepidus; who gave up their private friendfhips, and facrificed their particular connections,
to the fyftem of the compact of the Roman Triumvirate.
The King of Spain has gone much farther; for he has made
a kind of holocauft, or whole burnt-offering, of all the
interefts of the Spanifh nation, at the fhrine of family
ambition. He joined the French in the war againft England,
and ruined his army in Portugal; his fleet was deftroyed
at the Havanna; and, after the taking of that place, all
Spanifh America lay in a manner open, and almoft defencelefs, to the conquering fleets and armies of Britain.

Befides thefe involuntary loffes, the Spaniards were, in
confequence of the Family Compact, to lofe their independancy, their cuftoms, their manners, their language,
their drefs, and become Frenchmen; in order that their
Sovereign might be looked upon as a native of France,
and be acceptable to the French nation. Moreover the
Spaniards, in a courfe of years, muft, according to this
plan, lofe their trade and their wealth. For the trade and
wealth of Spain, and Spanifh America, being equally
open to the French as to the Spaniards themfelves, the

French,

French, being more numerous, more active and induſtrious, as well as more ſupple and inſinuating, will, in time, mono-polize the Spaniſh commerce, to the great diſadvantage of Spain, and of all the trading nations of Europe, who have hitherto ſent their manufactures, and had a ſhare in the Spaniſh trade. The French will want few manufactures, but their own, for ſupplying the conſumption.in Spain and Spaniſh America ; or they will have Eaſt India goods ſent from Manilla, in greater quantities than at preſent, rather than let their European neighbours come in for a part of the wealth of the Spaniſh Weſt Indies.

By ſome late edicts of the King of Spain, the ſale of wool and of raw ſilk is ſo reſtrained, that the whole trade in thoſe important articles may ſoon be monopolized by French factors ; and, what is aſtoniſhing, the manufac-tures of Spain are diſcouraged by the government, if they interfere with thoſe of France. Theſe are ſome of the effects of the Family Compact ; ſome others may be leſs perceptible at preſent, on account of the diſorder in the French finances, and the ambitious enterprizes of the Northern Powers. It is difficult to form reaſonable con-jectures of what may be the future conſequences of this extraordinary treaty ; becauſe there are but few treaties or tranſactions, in the hiſtory of former times, to which the Family Compact has any reſemblance.

The public articles of the Compact, in as much as they provide for the mutual naturalization of the ſubjects of both kingdoms, and the unnatural coalition of the power and intereſts of the two nations, which in themſelves are very oppoſite, ſeem to indicate a latent deſign, that the two kingdoms ſhould be governed by one Sovereign, if the ſucceſſion to both ſhould devolve on the ſame perſon. If

we

we contemplate the articles on another fide, and as they announce no other motives for this convention but the private affections of the two Monarchs for each other, and for the honour of their family, they are plainly taken from the fyftem of Eaftern defpotifm; according to which, the fubjects, and all that belongs to them, are confidered as the mere property of the Sovereign. And indeed fuch a vaft empire would arife from the union of France and Spain under one Sovereign, as, in the opinion of the author of the Spirit of Laws, would require that kind of arbitrary government, under which there are no intermediate powers; fuch as the immunities of the clergy, the privileges of the nobility, and the franchifes of different orders of citizens; all which, according to that fyftem, muft be annihilated, and all power and honours made to depend on the abfolute and immediate will of the defpot. Mr. Montefquieu has forewarned his countrymen againft this revolution in their government, and againft the defire of greatly extending the dominion of their Sovereign; which, he has foretold, would be the caufe of fuch a change in the conftitution of the French monarchy.

The plan alfo of the fecret articles of the Family Compact, on the hopes given to the Spanifh Royal Family of one day fucceeding to the Crown of France, was probably taken from Eaftern notions, and from a fimilar piece of policy of the Turkifh Emperors; who have brought, and long retained, the Crim Tartary, in a ftate of vaffallage, by a Family Compact with the Cham or Sovereign of that country; by which it was agreed, as Mr. Knowles informs us in his Hiftory of the Turks, *that the Turkifh empire, for want of heirs male of the Othman family, is affured, and as it were entailed, unto the Tartar Cham.* The Turkifh Sultan and

and the Tartar Cham being defcended from one common anceftor, the Cham looks upon the Sultan as his Chief, or the head of his family, and by primogeniture inheriting the rights of fatherhood from their patriarch or firft parent.

There is nothing that has contributed more to mifguide both kings and fubjects, in their ideas of civil government, than confounding the duties of the child with the duties of the fubject, by a fancied allufion between the power of the father and the power of the magiftrate. For as all right and property is underftood to be in the father, and the child has only the ufe of what the father allots for his fuftenance; fo, according to thefe principles, it is contended, that the Sovereign is the fole proprietor, and that the fubject has only what the civilians call the *ufus fructus*, during the will and pleafure of the patriarchal magiftrate.

From thefe mifconceived notions are derived the Family Compacts, and all thofe treaties which are contracted on other motives than the well-being of the people. The Othman Family Compact has long rendered the Crimea and the Crim Tartary dependant on the Turkifh Emperor; but yet it may happen that the Bourbon Family Compact may not be attended with the fame confequences in regard to Spain, as the wealth, the fituation, and other circumftances, of the Spanifh and Tartar nations, are very different. The Spaniards have already refifted againft one badge of flavery, the wearing the French drefs; and there are many events that may fruftrate the intent of the French Family Compact. The three fons of the late Dauphin are alive, notwithftanding the prognoftics of the phyficians. If they have male iffue, it may throw the profpect of inheriting the kingdom of France at fuch a diftance, as to be no longer an object of attention to the Princes of the Spanifh
Royal

Royal family. Moreover, they may difcover, that the will of Kings, however irrefiftible in their life-time, is often fet afide after their death; and that the law of fuc-ceffion to the kingdom of France, eftablifhed by the pre-fent Monarch, may be as little regarded as the laft will of Lewis XIV.

The neighbouring Powers would, for many reafons, op-pofe the folemn and public renunciation, made in the treaty of Utrecht, being annulled by a fecret convention. The French, on many occafions, have been remarkable for their averfion to be governed by foreigners; which has been prevented, in regard to the fucceffion to the Crown, by their Salic law. It is true, the letter of that law only excludes females from inheriting the kingdom, but the reafon of it, or the true caufe for continuing that antient regulation down to the prefent time, feems to be, becaufe the Princeffes marry into foreign families, and their children would be ftrangers to the genius and manners of the French nation; which, in the perfon of their Sovereign, would be very difagreeable to them. It cannot be for any fuppofed imbecility in the fex; becaufe the Dowager Queens have governed during the minority of their fons, and there are few Courts where the women have had greater influence. The males alfo have been excluded, who claimed in the right of females, as was the cafe of our King Edward the Third. The oftenfible or law-reafon given was, that as the Queen his mother could have no right, fhe could tranfmit none to her fon; but the true reafon feems to have been, that he was confidered as an alien by the generality of the French nation; and the Spanifh Princes would pro-bably meet with the fame oppofition in the minds of the people. It may alfo happen, that, if the prefent King of

Spain

Spain is not influenced by a view of the many advantages that would accrue to the Spanish monarchy by a lasting alliance with England, still a successor may see his interests in a different light, or he may be swayed by the sentiments of the most discerning part of his subjects: for the councils of the Sovereign, even in the most absolute governments, are sooner or later affected by the general sense of the nation.

This is the principal reason for addressing the public on this subject; because the merchants and others, who have an intercourse with the Spaniards, may have frequent opportunities of suggesting what is here alleged, and many other motives that may occur to them, for fixing a kind of national complaisance and good understanding between people who can become so many ways benefactors to each other. If unfortunately a war should break out, in pursuance of the scheme formed by the Family Compact, still the good will of the Spaniards might be cultivated, by compassion shewn to those who may be conquered or made prisoners, and by other acts of humanity, to which Englishmen are often well disposed. We might also represent to the Spaniards, that it was against the King, not against the Spanish nation, that we carried on the war; in a manner somewhat similar to the war of the King of Syria against Ahab King of Israel. The Syrians were ordered, not to consider the Israelites as their enemies, but to direct their force against Ahab their King, who had been deluded by his false prophets. So we may assure the Spaniards, that we are ever desirous of peace and harmony with them and that we consider their King, as he seems to consider himself, not as the head and representative of their nation, but as a Prince of the Bourbon family, who inherits the

G

Spanish

Spanish monarchy as a provifion made for a younger branch of the Bourbons; or, as the French would exprefs it, *La monarchie d'Efpagn n' eft que l'apanage d'un cadet de la maifon de Bourbon;* but that we have no enmity againft the people of Spain, and no ambition to poffefs any territory they are mafters of; that we are fenfible that the empires of Peru and Mexico would be our ruin, and the poffeffion of them would probably depopulate our country ftill more than it has the fouthern provinces of Spain, as our extenfive navigation, and the nature of our government, will not admit of the fame reftraints againft emigrations as are enacted in Spain; from whence no perfon can go to America without the King's licenfe. We might add, that we expect no fubjection or fubferviency on the part of Spain, but that each nation might treat according to the dignity of a fovereign and independant ftate; that we afk for nothing of the Spaniards but their friendfhip, and a mutual, well-regulated commerce, beneficial to both nations.

The fettlements in Falkland's Iflands, in Florida, and on the River Miffifippi, may be looked upon as precautions againft the too apparent intentions of the Family Compact, and the warlike preparations of the Court of Spain. If the Englifh nation and commerce were treated in a friendly manner, and according to that rank, in which a true regard to the interefts of the Spanifh monarchy ought to place them, the Spaniards might depend upon both the government, and the fubjects of Great Britain, contracting fentiments of reciprocal benevolence; and our naval power, which is now a fubject of alarm and jealoufy, would then be the protection of the vaft Spanifh American empire.

England

England has engaged in wars, and fpent her fterling millions, on the moft difinterefted principles of heroifm; there can then be no doubt, but that our brave country-men would exert their ftrength in favour of a nation, from whofe alliance and commerce they would draw great and perpetual advantages.

INTRODUCTION.

Of the moſt Southern Part of A M E R I C A, *deſcribed in the* M A P.

I DO not purpoſe to give an account of the kingdom of Chili, as Ovales has given an account of it already; but ſhall confine myſelf to thoſe parts I have ſeen, and to thoſe that are leaſt known in Europe.

The ſeacoaſt in the map is, for the moſt part, taken from Mr. D'Anville's map of South America, as improved by Mr. Bolton; Falkland's Iſlands, from the lateſt diſcoveries; and the Straits of Magellan, from Mr. Bernetti's map, who was chaplain in Mr. Bougainville's ſquadron.

I have made ſome alterations in the eaſtern ſeacoaſt, which I viewed in the year 1746; and about Cape St. Anthony, where I lived ſome years. In the deſcription of the inland country, I have in general followed my own obſervations; having travelled over great part of it, and traced the ſituation of places, and their diſtances, with the rivers, woods, and mountains. Where I could not penetrate, I have had accounts from the native Indians; and from Spaniſh captives, who had lived many years amongſt them, and afterwards obtained their liberty. Among many others, from whom I had my information, was the ſon of Captain Manſilla, of Buenos-Ayres, who

was

was fix years prifoner among the Tehuelhets, and who had travelled over the greateft part of their country; and like-wife the great Cacique Cangapol, who refided at Huichin, on the Black River. I have endeavoured to draw his like-nefs, as well as I could by memory. His figure and drefs are reprefented on the map, and thofe of his wife Huennee. This Chief, who was called by the Spaniards the Cacique Bravo, was tall and well-proportioned. He muft have been feven feet and fome inches in height; becaufe, on tiptoe, I could not reach to the top of his head. I was very well acquainted with him, and went fome journeys in his company. I do not recollect ever to have feen an Indian, that was above an inch or two taller than Cangapol. His brother, Saufimian, was but about fix feet high. The Patagonians, or Puelches, are a large bodied people; but I never heard of that gigantic race, which others have men-tioned, though I have feen perfons of all the different tribes of fouthern Indians.

All my own obfervations, and my inquiries of other perfons, oblige me to reprefent the country a great deal broader, from eaft to weft, than it appears in Mr. D'Anville's map; which I am not able to reconcile to the relations of the Indians, nor to what I obferved myfelf, with refpect to the diftances of places. Even in the Spanifh country, he is I think miftaken, in making the diftance between Cordova and Santa Fe forty leagues lefs than it is in reality. The road is an entire plain, with not fo much as a hillock, between thefe two cities; yet no poftboy will undertake to go it in lefs than four or five days; and the poftboys, in that country, generally travel twenty leagues or more in a day.

The

The journey between thefe two cities I have myfelf taken four times, as well as between both of them and Buenos-Ayres.

I do not believe that any able perfon has made an obfervation of the longitude in thefe parts, to be depended upon, in order to fix the difference of meridian of thefe places of the fouthern hemifphere. And the miftakes of geographers, in reprefenting this country narrower than it really is, may be owing to the difficulty of keeping a true reckoning in failing round Cape Horn; which is occafioned by the velocity and variety of the currents: A particular account of which may be found in the Englifh tranflation of Don Ulloa's Voyage to South America, vol. II. b. iii. c. 2.

C H A P-

CHAPTER I.

Of the Soil and Produce of the most southern Part of
A M E R I C A.

T HE district of the city of St. Jago del Estero, in the province of Tucuman, is a flat, dry, sandy soil. The greatest part of it is covered with thick woods, which begin at fifty leagues to the south, and reach to the district of Tucuman, which is thirty leagues to the north of St. Jago. They extend to the eastward of the Rio Dulce, near twenty miles, and, to the westward, as far as the Chaco, which is above sixty miles.

There are so few open spots in this district, and those which are open so frequently overflowed by the rivers Dulce and Salado (the sweet and salt rivers) that the inhabitants are obliged to fell the woods, to get sufficient space to sow their chacras. Behind the woods, to the eastward, towards the mountains of the Rioia, and those of the vale of Catamarca, are vast plains, where there is plenty of pasture, but without any fresh water whatsoever, except what is collected in lakes in rainy seasons; and when these fail, there is great danger of perishing with thirst, in travelling over them. The great number of crosses which have been erected, and are now to be seen in these plains, are proofs,

I

how

how many have fallen a prey to their rafhnefs, in venturing upon fo hazardous a journey. This vaft country extends to near eighty leagues, from the mountains of Cordova to thofe of the vale of Catamarca, and is called the Travefia of Quilino and Ambergafta.

Notwithftanding thefe difadvantages, the foil is not unfruitful, when duly cultivated, and produces water and mufk melons, of a prodigious fize, and the beft flavoured of any that grow in thefe countries. Thofe of Tucuman are larger, but, from the extreme moiftnefs of the foil, are not fo well tafted. Corn is alfo raifed here in great quantities, and fent to Cordova and Buenos-Ayres. Cotton thrives very well; and indigo was formerly a great commodity in this country, but, through the neglect of the inhabitants, is entirely loft. A fmall quantity of cochineal is gathered from a kind of low, thorny opuntia, that fpreads itfelf upon the ground, and grows wild in the woods; and much more might be taken, if it was cultivated, and prepared in the fame manner as in Quito, and other parts of Peru. The foil, with due care and cultivation, will alfo produce peaches, figs, and dates.

The fruits which grow wild are the algarrova, the miftol, the channar, and the molie; with fome others of leffer note.

The algarrova is a large tree in this country, about the bignefs of a middle-fized oak. It's timber is ftrong, durable, and largely grained. It's leaves are fmall and fcalloped; many of them growing together on one common ftalk, near and oppofite to each other; fo that ten or twenty of them feem to compofe one leaf, as in the fpruce pine. It's flowers are fmall, of a faint white colour, and grow in clufters, like currants, but fmaller and thicker.

Thefe

Thefe are fucceeded by large, long pods, like thofe of peas, but not fo broad. They are of two kinds, white and black; the latter is narrower, but fomewhat fweeter. Before it is arrived at maturity, it is green, and has a ftrong aftringency, and a remarkable roughnefs on the tongue; but when it is ripe, has an uncommon fweetnefs, and a ftrong, unpleafant fmell, like that of bugs. This tree grows in very great plenty, and is a kind of fweet acacia, being like to the acacia arabica. The inhabitants make a confiderable harveft of the fruit, which is a great part of their fuftenance. They reduce it to flour, and fometimes mix it with that of Indian wheat: when diluted with cold water, they call it anapa. The flour alone, which is very gummy, and fticks together, they prefs into cakes, or fquare boxes, and preferve it for food: this they call patay. Of the pods bruifed they make a very ftrong drink, or chica, by letting it ftand, from twelve to twenty-four hours, infufed in a fufficient quantity of cold water; in which time it ferments, becomes very ftrong and heady, and occafions heavy drunkennefs. A great quantity of proof fpirit might be drawn from this chica; but the inhabitants are not fufficiently fkilful for that purpofe. More to the fouthward, this tree does not grow fo large, and in the country of the Tehuelhets, it dwindles to a fmall fhrub, not more than a yard in height. I have feen the fruit of this tree given, in confumptions arifing from profufe fweats, and hectics, either in patay or chica, with great fuccefs; nor are thofe diforders common among the people who ufe it for food.

There is another fpecies of this kind of tree, which I take to be the true acacia of the Arabs. It's leaves are like thofe of the algarrova, but the flower and fruit are very different. The flowers are of a fine yellow colour, very

fmall

fmall, grow together in a round heap, and have a very aromatic fmell. The pods are thicker, very black, with feeds like lentils, but harder. They have a gummy quality, a ftrong, aftringent tafte, and, with copperas, make a black ink, dying cloth and linen black; for which purpofe they are ufed by the inhabitants. The wood is more firm, and it's colour is of a deeper red, than that of the algarrova, and it weeps a gum, exactly the fame as the common gum arabic.

There is a third fort, that is not fo lofty, whofe pod is of a dull red, inclining fomewhat to brown; it is neither aftringent nor fweet; but the natives make a chicha of it, with which they cure themfelves of the *lues venerea*. It's operation is fudorific,. and I have fometimes known cures performed by it, which in England would have required a falivation.

I have alfo feen a fourth kind of thefe pods, which came from the Chaco, and were much larger and ftronger, and their colour was of a deeper red, than any of the former. They were very aftringent and balfamic, had a ftrong fmell, like cyprefs wood, and were the fruit (as the miffionary who brought them affured me) of a large, thorny tree, without leaves. I believe that they are balfamic, aftringent vulneraries, and might be of great ufe in phyfic, at leaft in outward applications.

The miftol is, in this country, a low, knotty, crooked tree; in hotter countries it grows taller and more ftraight; and in the colder parts, to the fouth of St. Jago, it does not grow at all. The Indians ufe it for their lances, it being a very heavy and tough wood. It bears a fruit of a red colour, as big as a chefnut; the cortical part of which is very thin, and it contains a large, hard ftone. The natives eat the
rind,

rind, and the small quantity of flesh that is under it, and likewise make a chica of it, which is very sweet.

The channar, in the warmer climates, is a thick, tall tree, though not so large as here, more to the south. It's branches are very crooked and thorny. It's trunk is always green, and has a thin bark, like parchment, that dries, peels off, and is succeeded by a new one. It makes good fire and charcoal. It's wood is hard and firm, inclining to a yellow colour. The Indians use it chiefly for stirrups, though it seems capable of other uses, such as building, &c. It's leaves are small and oval; it's fruit is like that of the mistol, though less; neither is it so sweet, or of so red a colour. It's uses are the same as those of the mistol.

The molie is a great tree, not to be found to the south of the Province of Tucuman. The timber of this tree is of a very fine grain, and extremely beautiful; but of little use, on account of it's being so very subject to be worm-eaten. There are two sorts of it; one, which has a leaf of the bigness of a bay leaf, and bearing a resemblance to it; the other is exactly the same, only smaller. They are both evergreens, and their leaves, when bruised, serve to tan the fine goatskin leather, made in this country. Their trunks weep a considerable quantity of gum, which is used as incense, being very odoriferous. That with the larger leaves bears great plenty of a black fruit, which, when ripe, has a skin of a very light blue colour, almost white. It is about the size of a currant, and many of them grow in a cluster, like cherries. They are even sweeter than the al-garrova; and, being boiled in water, they produce an extract or syrup, very sweet, and hot in the mouth; being steeped in water, they make a chicha, much stronger than that of the algarrova, both in taste and smell. The drunken-

K

nefs

nefs it occafions generally lafts two or three days, and gives a wild, glaring appearance, to the eyes of thofe who are intoxicated with it: a certain proof of the ftrength and quantity of the fpirit it contains.

There are many other very beautiful and ufeful trees, and of a vaft height, that grow chiefly in the deep vales, and breaks of the high mountains: among which are the white and red quiabrahacho, the viraro, the lapacho, the cedar, the timbo, the wild walnut-tree; together with the laurel and the willow. Thefe laft grow there very tall and thick, but are not of much ufe.

The white and red quiabrahacho (or break-axe) fo called from their extreme hardnefs, grow in the woods, in the plain countries northward of Cordova. In St. Jago they grow to the height of eight or ten yards, very ftraight, and proportionably thick. The former of thefe trees has leaves refembling thofe of our box, but fomething larger, with a fharp, thorny point: the wood being alfo like boxwood, but of a red colour at the heart. It is very good timber, of a fine grain, but very brittle, hard to work, and exceedingly heavy. The latter is a different kind of tree. It's leaves grow in the manner of thofe of the yew tree; it is more lofty and heavier than the white quiabrahacho; and it's timber is as red as blood, and can only be worked while it is green; for after it has been kept fome time, it becomes fo very hard, that no tool can touch it. In hardnefs and colour it bears fo ftrong a refemblance to red marble, that it is a difficult matter to diftinguifh them.

The viraro affords a wood of a white colour, like our elm, and is ufed for beams, or any other fuch purpofes. It is very durable, and is eafy to be worked.

The

The lapacho is one of the moſt valuable timber trees of theſe countries. I never ſaw it growing, but have often ſeen large beams, &c. of it, of eight or nine yards in length, which were to be ſent into Spain, for the uſe of their oil-mills, to cruſh the olives. The timber is of a duſky, green colour, has a good grain, and is not ſo brittle as the quiabrahacho, but is very hard and heavy.

The cedars are like ours. The timbo is a kind of coarſe cedar, which grows on the banks of rivers.

The wild walnut-trees are very large and lofty. I have ſeen ſome that were brought, worked and ſquared, from Tucuman, which meaſured twelve yards in length. They bear no fruit, and their leaf is like that of our walnut-tree, but ſomething bigger. In ſome of the deep vallies among the mountains, I have ſeen cedars and wild walnut-trees, that I judged might meaſure from fifteen to twenty yards in height, as ſtraight as an arrow. All theſe grow wild; with many other excellent timber trees, almoſt all of which bear thorns. Among which it may not be improper to mention the lanza; ſo called, becauſe of this the natives make ſpears and lances. This tree is of a yellow colour, very ſtraight, is excellent timber, and makes the beſt axle-trees for carts and coaches.

The inhabitants cultivate many fruit trees which grow wild in Paraguay, as lemons, and oranges both ſweet and ſour. Peaches, both cultivated and wild, are in great abundance. In Cordova and Mendoza, they have apples and pears of many kinds, pomegranates, apricots, plums, and cherries. In ſome places, figs almoſt grow wild, or at leaſt with very little culture; and alſo the Indian fig. This country, in ſome parts of it, produces vines; which in Mendoza, Rioia, and San Juan, are very much cultivated;

as alfo in the vale of Catamarca, and at Cordova, where there are fome few vineyards. The wine which is produced is partly for private ufe, and partly to fell at Buenos-Ayres, Tucuman, Salta, Injuy, &c. This commodity is fometimes very cheap, and would be much more fo, was it not for the heavy taxes it pays, in the cities to which it is fent.

Corn, and almoft all manner of grain, is cultivated, and flourifhes, in the jurifdictions of Cordova, St. Jago, and Rioia, when it can be watered; and likewife in Buenos-Ayres and Santa Fe, if the year is not too dry. This article might be in great plenty; and very great quantities might be produced more to the fouth; but the Indians do not fow. The Moluches alone clean the earth a little, without ploughing, and fet as much as they are able to cut with their knives. In Tucuman, the country is too moift for corn; but the inhabitants gather great crops of maize, or Indian wheat, which they exchange for corn with thofe of St. Jago.

One of the chief articles of commerce at St. Jago is wax and honey; which are found, in great plenty, in the vaft woods on the other fide of the river Salado. Great quantities of thefe commodities are taken from the hollow parts of decayed trees, and fold all over the neighbouring provinces. There is likewife a kind of honey, called alpamifqua, made by a very fmall bee. It is worked in holes under ground, in ftony countries; it's tafte is a four fweet; it is very diuretic, and extremely good for the ftone and gravel.

Another, and a very confiderable product of this country (though as yet unnoticed) is falt petre; which might be gathered in vaft quantities, if diligently attended to; as there is an immenfe tract of falt territory, of about two hundred

or

or two hundred and fifty leagues in length, and from forty to fifty leagues wide. It begins at about twelve leagues to the north of the mountains of the Vuulcan, and extends itself in breadth to Cape St. Anthony. It takes in all the jurifdiction of Buenos-Ayres, and the fouth and weft fide of the river of Plata, and, leaving Cordova to the weft, runs through all the territory of Santa Fe, as far as the city of the Corientes, at the junction of 'the famous rivers of Paraguay and Parana. It's breadth is here fo very extenfive, as to comprehend all that part of the diftrict of St. Jago, which lies to the weft of the river Dulce, and all the plain country of Rioia, as far as the limits of the vale of Catamarca. This is evident, from the brackifh tafte of all the brooks and rivers which pafs through this falt foil; whofe waters are not fit to be drunk, till they enter the Parana. All the fprings in this great tract of country are more or lefs falt. But the rivers which flow from the mountains of Cordova, Tucuman, Choromoros, and Anconquixa, are excellent water where they firft break forth, and continue fo for many leagues; when they either reach the Parana, or are fwallowed up in the falt lakes. A confiderable quantity of falt is made of the earth, for private ufe, in the city of the Affumption, in Paraguay; but it appears in the greateft plenty in the neighbourhood of the Rioia and St. Jago. After a fhower of rain, the earth becomes white with the faltpetre, and is extremely chilling to the feet. It may then, with a brufh or a feather, be gathered in great abundance, with very little earth; as likewife by taking the rain water from the lakes. The people of thefe parts gather little more than what they ufe for the making of gunpowder; which is prepared chiefly for their feafts. I have frequently bought fmall quantities of it, of about twenty pounds

L

weight,

weight, coarfely purified from the filth; all in fmall cryftal cylinders, without any cubes; which proves that it is unmixed with fal gem; which our faltpetre is not fo free from. This difcovery might be attended with great advantages, if proper attention was paid to it; as the faltpetre might be carried in boats, by the river Salado, to Santa Fe, and from thence, by the Parana, to Buenos-Ayres.

The greateft commerce of this country is that of cattle. There are every where very numerous flocks of fheep; and, at my firft going thither, the horned cattle were fo abundant, that (befides the herds of tame cattle) they ran, in vaft droves, wild and without owners, in the plains on both fides of the rivers Parana, Uruguay, and the river of Plata; and covered all the plains of Buenos-Ayres, Mendoza, Santa Fe, and Cordova. But the covetoufnefs and neglect of the Spaniards have deftroyed fuch vaft numbers of the wild cattle, that, had it not been for the providential care of fome few particular people, flefh would, at this time, have been extremely dear in thofe parts. On my firft arrival in this country, not a year paffed, but from five to eight fhips fet fail from Buenos-Ayres, laden chiefly with hides. Immenfe flaughters were made, without more gain than the fat, fuet, and hides; the flefh being left to rot. The annual confumption of cattle, flain in this manner alone, in the jurifdiction of this one city and Santa Fe, did not amount to lefs than fome hundreds of thoufands. Nor is the practice entirely laid afide at this time. Yet, not-withftanding, cattle are cheap; and, even in Cordova, bullocks are fold for two dollars a head; but formerly they would not have been eftimated at more than half the prefent price.

There

There is likewife great plenty of tame horfes, and a prodigious number of wild ones. The price of a two or three
year old colt is half a dollar, or about two fhillings and
fourpence ; of a horfe fit for fervice, two dollars ; and of
a mare, three rials, and fometimes only two. The wild
horfes have no owners, but wander, in great troops, about
thofe vaft plains, which are terminated, to the eaftward, by
the province of Buenos-Ayres and the ocean, as far as the
mouth of the Red River ; to the weftward, by the mountains
of Chili and the firft Defaguadero ; to the north, by the
mountains of Cordova, Yacanto, and Rioia ; and to the
fouth, by the woods which are the boundaries of the
Tehuelhets and Diuihets. They go from place to place,
againft the current of the winds ; and, in an inland expedition which I made in 1744, being in thefe plains for the
fpace of three weeks, they were in fuch vaft numbers, that,
during a fortnight, they continually furrounded me. Sometimes they paffed by me, in thick troops, on full fpeed, for
two or three hours together ; during which time, it was with
great difficulty that I and the four Indians, who accom-
panied me on this occafion, preferved ourfelves from being
run over and trampled to pieces by them. At other times,
I have paffed over this fame country, and have not feen
any of them.

This great plenty of horfes and horned cattle is fuppofed
to be the reafon, why the Spaniards and the Indians do not
cultivate their lands with that care and induftry which they
require, and that idlenefs prevails fo much among them.
Any one can with eafe have, or train up, a troop of horfes ;
and being accoutred with his knife and lazo, or fnare of
hiderope, he has wherewith to get his livelihood ; cows
and calves being in great abundance, and out of their owners
fight ;

fight; fo that it is an eafy matter to kill them, without being difcovered : which practice is very much followed.

There have been various attempts towards the difcovery
of mines in this country; but they have all proved abor-
tive. Some traces of a gold mine were difcovered, in the
jurifdiction of Cordova, in the vale of Punillia; but, after
much labour and expenfe, the quantity of gold was very in-
confiderable, and the undertakers were ruined. The fame
fate attended the workers of another gold mine, found
near the mouth of the Plata, in the mountains near Maldonado; which was abandoned from the fame motives as
the former. About ten years ago, there was a great noife
about filver mines near the mountain of Anconquixa, and
at firft fome quantity of filver was obtained. With this
encouragement, the governor of the province interefted
himfelf in it, notice was given of it to the King of Spain,
and many expended their fortunes in the undertaking; but,
after two years failure, it was given up, like the two former.

A few years ago, there was another difcovery made of
fome filver mines, near Mendoza, at the foot of the Cordillera; which, after fome trials, yielded a large quantity
of ore. The undertakers were at a very great expenfe, in
procuring engines, and all the other apparatus neceffary to
carry on the work; but, before I left the country, fome
very unfavourable accounts had been received concerning
thefe mines: fo that I cannot pretend to determine whether
they have fucceeded or not. Even the famous filver mines
of Potofi are very confiderably diminifhed. The quantity
of ore taken from thence is decreafed near two thirds, and
the Indians who ufed to work them are almoft all of them
deftroyed, for want of a good police; and befides, many

of

of the mines are overflowed, and are thereby rendered ufe-lefs and unprofitable.

There is a great probability, that there might be found as many gold and filver mines, in the country of the Indian Moluches, on the eaft fide of the Cordillera, as have been to the weft; but the Indians pay no attention to fuch difco-veries, and the Spaniards are afraid to pafs thefe mountains, to make any trial, left they fhould be attacked by the Indians.

There are likewife, in thefe parts, various drugs; which might be very profitable, if the inhabitants thought proper to attend to them.

In the jurifdiction of Tucuman, and the city of the Seven Currents, there are great quantities of guaiacum, or holy wood, and of dragon's blood; which laft is a very valuable commodity. It flows from the tree upon incifion, and refembles, upon infpiffation, real blood; as well in colour, as in confiftence. It hardens, with boiling, or af-ter long keeping, to a kind of rofin; and becomes of a liver-colour, much darker than our officinal dragon's blood. It is likewife much more aftringent.

The balfam of caaci flows from a tree upon incifion, and is fometimes got by boiling it's boughs, very much bruifed It is a hard gum, of the turpentine kind, but of a white colour, when got by boiling; otherwife, it is yellow and clear. It is a moft excellent incarnating medicine for wounds, and a fine vulnerary taken internally.

Two Indians were feverally wounded by a narrow lance, in the epigaftric region, juft beneath the xiphoide cartilage. The points of the weapons came out on one fide of the back-bone; a fmall degree higher in the one cafe than the other. What they drank iffued immediately out of the wounds.

M

They

They suffered great pain, and had frequent lypothymies (or faintings) and cold, clammy sweats. I was used to apply this balsam externally, mixed with deer's suet and marrow; but in these cases, the wounds were closed. I gave it them internally; and they took a small quantity of it, about the bigness of a hazel nut, three times a day, and sometimes oftener in a less quantity. I had no other medicine in those desarts to give them, that could be of any service in their case. However, they were both restored to a perfect state of health and strength; the one, in six weeks, the other, in about three months.

I mention these two cases as very particular ones, the stomach having been pierced before and behind; a case generally esteemed mortal by the faculty. The narrowness of the perforations (made by the narrow blade of a tuck, or small sword, converted into a lance) was, I imagine, the reason of these cures being so soon completed.

The balsam, or rather extract, called aquaaribaigh, is got by boiling a plant, which is a kind of shrub lentiscus. In external applications, it is a good cleanser and digestive, and likewise breeds a good cicatrix. It is very efficacious, internally, in hemorrhages, dysenteries, and catarrhs; being an agglutinant, and an astringent, as well as a balsamic.

The gum isica flows from a tree, and is gathered in Paraguay. It is called likewise trementine, that is, turpentine; but it seems to be a species of gum elemi, though much hotter; and, when applied alone, it will raise blisters. It's chief use, in this country, is to make plasters for the sciatica; which it frequently cures. When tempered with an equal portion of wax or tallow, it makes a pretty good liniment of arceus; and is a good cephalic plaster, applied with oxycroceum, to the feet; which it never fails to keep

warm

warm. This is of great fervice to the Indians, and inhabitants in general; as they are very fubject to obftructions in the liver, arifing from drinking too large quantities of cooling liquors; and thefe diforders are attended with a great coldnefs in the feet.

The contrayerva root is in great abundance. And in fome parts of the mountains of Cordova and Yacanto, the valerian and meum roots grow in great quantities, of a much larger fize, and of a ftronger fmell, than any I have feen in Europe. There are roots of the valerian as thick as a man's arm. They have the fame kind of fmell as ours, but, as I have juft before obferved, much ftronger. The leaves of the meum are very large: It grows to a yard in height. The flowers are white, and clufter together, in a conic form, four or five inches high. It's ufe is well known, in nervous diforders and epilepfies.

There are brought from the Guaranies two forts of roots, of a plant, or flag, which the natives call fchynant; but, though they bear the fame name, they differ very much from each other. The one has all the appearance of the common calamus aromaticus, though it is fomewhat ftronger, both in tafte and fmell, and not fo large. The other has very fmall, round roots, about half an inch in length; very brittle, eafy to be pounded fine, and of the fame colour as the contrayerva. It has a very hot, fpicy, aromatic tafte, and, when taken inwardly, is a very good medicine in all cold affections of the brain and nerves.

Ginger likewife grows in thefe parts. But the commodity which might turn to the greateft advantage, if the proper methods of preparing it were difcovered, is a kind of tea, which I found about two years before my departure from this place. It bears an exact refemblance

to

to the herb fo called which comes from China; for, on putting fome leaves of both forts into boiling water, I could not difcover, when they were difplayed, any difference, either in their fhape, or the difpofition of their veins and fibrous parts. I found this tea plant, in very great quantities, in different vales; at the foot of the mountains of Cordova and Yacanto, near the mountains of Achala, and in the vallies of Calamochita; and I have been informed, that, nearer Peru, in Tucuman, Salta, &c. it grows in greater plenty.

It is a fhrub, from a yard to above two yards high. It's trunk feldom exceeds an inch in thicknefs, and is often lefs. It has no fuckers near the root; but many long branches. It's leaves grow by three and three, in the manner of trefoil; they are of a beautiful green, and very fmooth. It fhoots out a long fpike of blue flowers, fomething like lavender, but not fo long, nor fo well fcented. To each of thefe flowers fucceeds a fmall hufk, each of which contains a feed, not bigger than a third part of a lentil, fhaped like a kidneybean. After it is dry, on infufing it in water, it tinges the water in the fame manner as green tea. It's tafte and flavour are exactly the fame, except that it is fome-what ftronger, and is not fo rough; but this difference is moft probably owing to the frefhnefs of it when gathered, or perhaps may arife from the different method of preparing it, or from not drying it on copper-plates, as is faid to be done in China. In the drying, I could not make it become twifted and fhrivelled, like the oriental tea.

I found likewife a leffer kind of this plant, both with refpect to it's height, and the fize of it's leaves.

There is yet another fpecies of it, which grows in Chili. This has a round feed, without the hufk; the flowers are
yellow,

yellow, and do not grow in a fpike; and the leaf is not fo fmooth as that of the former, and is of a lighter green. On infufion, it gives a deeper tinge. The tafte is much the fame as that of the other fort, but not quite fo pleafant, having a fmall degree of faintnefs in it's flavour. The Indian name is culem. The inhabitants of Cordova call theirs alvanhacca del campo, that is, wild bafil; but this is a name given at random, to a plant, which bears no refemblance to the bafil, either wild or cultivated; that being an herb, and not a tree.

As I and feveral of my acquaintance gathered fome bags of this tea, and freely diftributed it to many perfons, I had an opportunity of trying it's effects; and found that it created a good appetite and digeftion, cured many head-achs and inveterate apepfias (want of appetite), and anorexias (want of digeftion), which had not yielded to any other re-medies; in thefe particulars far excelling the tea of China. It is very remarkable, that, in the parts where this tea plant grows, there is the fame kind of ftone as that of which the China ware is made.

CHAPTER II.

A Defcription of the Indian Country, with it's Vales, Mountains, Rivers, &c.—Great River La Plata, with it's Branches, Fifh, and Ports.

THAT part of the jurifdiction of Cordova, which lies to the fouth of the Rio Segundo, or Second River, was formerly the country of a great party of the northern Puelches, and reaches above fifty leagues, entering into the jurifdiction of Buenos-Ayres be-yond Cruzalta. When I firft went into thofe parts, I met

fome

troops of thefe Indians, ftill inhabiting the banks of the Second and Third Rivers; and there were fome few of them on the Fourth and Fifth Rivers. All the country which lies between the Second and Third Rivers is about twelve leagues over, and moftly woody; but, on approaching the Third River, the wood ceafes. The rivers that wafh this country all come from the high mountains of Yacanto, Champachin, and Achala; which are little inferior in height to the Andes of Chili, and are a kind of branches of thofe of Peru. All thefe rivers, except the Third River, after paffing through the breaks in the mountains of Cordova, and rufhing into the plains, in a few leagues lofe their fweetnefs, become falt, grow lefs and lefs by the drynefs of the fandy foil, and are finally fwallowed up in fome lake.

The Rio Tercero, or Third River, the moft confiderable of them all, before it paffes the mountains of Cordova where it has a great fall) is increafed by the acceffion of the rivers Champachin, Gonfales, Del Medio, Quillimfa, Cachu-Corat, La Cruz, Luti, and Del Sauce; but coming to the plains, part of which are very fandy, during a dry feafon it difappears under the ground, and breaks out again at fome diftance. In times of rain it increafes very much, and brings down, in it's rapid current, great quantities of wood. It makes many windings, enclofing large fields. It's banks, for more than twenty leagues after it leaves the mountains, are full of high willow trees. The country through which it flows breeds excellent cattle, being fine pafture and corn land, and in fome places produces melilot, and a kind of woody farfaparilla. At the end of twenty leagues it grows falt, but is not fo very bad as to be unfit for drinking. In this manner it takes it's courfe to the Cruzalta, where it is called Carcaranna, from it's many windings,

and

and paffes on, running from N. N. W. to S. S. E. till it enters the Parana, at the Rincon, or corner, of Gaboto, about eighteen leagues from Santa Fe..

There is nothing particular in the Rivers Quarto and Quinto ; their produce is much the fame as that of the former, except that there is a greater fcarcity of wood in the countries through which they pafs. Their fields are ftocked with cattle, and are fit for tillage. The River Quinto, when it overflows, has a communication by chan-nels with the River Saladillo, which difcharges itfelf into the River of Plata.

Between this country and the plains of St. Juan and Mendoza (the habitation of the fecond divifion of the northern Puelches, or Taluhets) are the mountains of Cor-dova and Yacanto. They form a continued chain, with very bad paffes, through breaks of hills, and over afcents and ridges, which are very fteep, and unfit for wheel car-riages. The tops of thefe ridges are from fixteen to twenty leagues diftant from each other. The intervening country contains many fpacious and fruitful vallies, watered with brooks and rivulets, and beautified with hills and rifing grounds. Thefe vallies produce many kinds of fruit trees, as peaches, apples, cherries, and plums ; and alfo corn, where the land is cultivated : but they are more particularly famous for breeding cattle, fheep, and horfes, and efpecially mules. The greateft part of thefe laft, which pafs yearly over to Peru, are bred in this country, and are it's greateft riches, as they bring into it filver and gold, from the mines of Potofi, Lipes, and all Peru.

On the weftern fkirts of the mountains of Yacanto, or Sacanto, there are many farms belonging to the Spaniards, who have been allured thither by the fertility of the foil,
which

which is capable of all kinds of hufbandry, and is well watered by the rivulets which flow down from the mountains; and alfo by the facility of breeding cattle; there being few woods, except fuch as are neceffary for fuel and building. And befides, the fecurity from the annoyance of the Indians is another great inducement to fettle there, as they infeft thofe only, who live more to the fouth.

All the reft of the country to the weftward, between thefe mountains and the firft river Defaguadero, confifts of plains, with little water but what the brooks afford. It contains abundance of fine paftures, but is unpeopled. Sometimes indeed the Taluhets and Picunches go thither, in fmall troops, to hunt wild mares, or rob paffengers and waggons, which are paffing from Buenos-Ayres to San Juan and Mendoza.

This country affords little for exportation to Europe, except bull and cow hides, and fome tobacco, which grows very well in Paraguay; but it is of the greateft importance to the Spaniards, becaufe all the mules, or the greateft part of them, which are ufed in Peru, come from Buenos-Ayres and Cordova, and fome few from Mendoza; without which they would be totally difabled from carrying on any traffic, or having any communication with the neighbouring countries; as the high and rugged mountains of Peru are impaffable but by mules, and in that country they cannot breed thefe animals. Thofe alfo which go thither are in general fhort-lived on account of their hard labour, the badnefs of the roads, and the want of paftures. So that the lofs of this country might draw after it the lofs of Peru and Chili. The road from Buenos-Ayres to Salta is fit for wheel carriages; but the mules, which are driven from that place and Cordova, are obliged, after fo long a journey, to

reft

reſt a year in Salta, before they can paſs to Potoſi, Lipes, or Cuſco.

The people of theſe countries are very indifferent ſoldiers, and ſo diſpleaſed with the Spaniſh government, loſs of trade, the dearneſs of all European goods, and, above all, ſo many exorbitant taxes, &c. that they would be glad to be ſubject to any other nation, who would deliver them from their preſent oppreſſion. Yet, notwithſtanding, all this country is without any other guard, than a few regular troops in Buenos-Ayres and Montevideo; and if theſe two places were once taken, the taking of the reſt might be accompliſhed by only marching over it; in which any enemy would be aſſiſted by the natives of the country. The loſs of theſe two places would deprive the Spaniards of the only ports they have in theſe ſeas, where their ſhips, which are to paſs Cape Horn to the South Seas, can receive any ſuccour. Before the expulſion of the Jeſuits from the miſſions of Paraguay, they might have had very conſiderable ſuccours from the Indian Guaranies, who were armed and diſciplined, and who helped to ſubject the rebellious inſurgents of Paraguay, and to drive the Portugueſe out of the colony of Saint Sacrament, and were the greateſt defence of this important country.

That part of the Cordillera which lies weſt of Mendoza is of a vaſt height, and always covered with ſnow; from whence all this chain of mountains is called by the Indians Pſen Mahuiſau, or Snowy Mountain; or Liu, or Lio Mahuiſau, i. e. White Mountain. You paſs ſome leagues through very pleaſant vallies, encompaſſed with high hills, before you come to the greateſt ridge, which is very high and ſteep, with frequent frightful and deep precipices; and in ſome places the road is ſo very narrow and dangerous, on account

O

of

of many huge, prominent rocks, that there is scarce room
enough for a loaded mule to pass along. The hollows are
never without snow, even during the summer, and in the
winter there is great danger of being frozen to death.
Many have lost their lives, by attempting to pass them before the snows were in some degree melted. At the bottom
of these precipices, there are many brooks and rivers,
which are as it were imprisoned, between high, perpendicular banks; and so narrow is the space between them, in
some places, that one might leap from one side to the other;
but it is impossible to descend them. These rivers and
brooks take many windings within the hills and precipices,
till they break out into the plains, where they compleat the
bulk of greater rivers. To ascend, and pass over the great
ridge, is commonly one day's journey, at Mendoza and
Coquimbo, and much the same in other places, according
to the information I have received.

Thefe hills produce very large and lofty pine trees.
Their growth is like those of Europe, but their wood is
more solid and harder than ours; it is very white, and
makes excellent masts, as well as other materials for ship
building, and is very durable; so that, as Ovales remarks,
ships built in the South Seas often last forty years. The fruit
is bigger; the head that produces it being twice as large as
those which the Spanish pines bear; and the pine-nuts are
as big as dates, with a very slender shell. The fruit is long
and thick, with four blunt corners, as big as two almonds.
By boiling these fruits or kernels, they make provision for
long journies, or to keep at home. Prepared in this manner, they have something of a mealiness, and taste very like
a boiled almond, but not so oily. This tree produces a
considerable quantity of turpentine, which forms itself into

a mass,

a maſs, ſomething harder and drier than our roſin, but much more clear and tranſparent, though not ſo yellow. The Spaniards call, and uſe it as incenſe; but that is a miſtake, as it has no other fragrance than that of roſin, only ſomething finer.

The vales at the foot of the Cordillera are in ſome places very fertile, watered with brooks or rivers, and, when cultivated, produce good corn, and a variety of fruits. Apple trees grow there wild, in great abundance; and the Indians make a kind of cyder, for preſent uſe, being ignorant how to preſerve it.

The volcanoes, or fiery mountains, of which there are many on this ſide of the Cordillera, may vie with Veſuvius, Mont-Gibello, or any of thoſe which we know of in Europe, for their ſize and furious eruptions. Being in the Vuulcan, below Cape St. Anthony, I was witneſs to a vaſt cloud of aſhes being carried by the winds, and darkening the whole ſky. It ſpread over great part of the juriſdiction of Buenos-Ayres, paſſed the River of Plata, and ſcattered it's contents on both ſides of the river, in ſo much that the graſs was covered with aſhes. This was cauſed by the eruption of a volcano near Mendoza; the winds carrying the light aſhes to the incredible diſtance of three hundred leagues or more.

The country of Buenos-Ayres, the antient habitation of the Chechehets, is ſituated on the ſouth ſide of the River of Plata. The coaſt here is wet and low, with many bogs and marſhes. The waterſide is covered with wood, which ſerves for fuel. Theſe marſhes reach, from the banks, till you come to the riſing grounds; which are alſo in ſome parts very boggy; being a clay, with very little depth of ſoil to cover it, till you go farther into the country; where
the

the foil is deeper. The country is every where flat, with fmall rifing grounds; and it is very furprifing, that in all this vaft jurifdiction,· in that of Santa Fe, and of St. Jago del Eftero, there is not to be found one ftone, which is the natural produce of the country: and this is the cafe as far as the mountains of the Vuulcan, Tandit, and Cayru, to the fouth eaft of Buenos-Ayres.

The country which is between Buenos-Ayres, and the river Saladillo (the limit and boundary of the Spanifh government to the fouth of this province) is entirely a plain, without fo much as one tree or rifing ground, till you come to the banks of this river, which is about twenty-three leagues from the Spanifh fettlements. This country is near twenty leagues broad, from N. E. to S. W. and is bounded by the ftraggling villages of the Matanza and Magdalen. To the north of the Saladillo there are many great lakes, fome bogs, and hollow vales. The lakes I am acquainted with are thofe of the Reduction, Sauce, Vitel, Chafcamuz, Cerrillos, and Lobos. To the fouth eaft, there is a long and narrow lake of fweet water, near the river Borombon, which is very rare in this country; it is eight leagues diftant from the neareft Spanifh fettlement. About fix leagues farther is the great river, or rather lake of Borombon; which is formed by the overflowing of the lakes of the Reduction, Sauce, Vitel, and Chafcamuz, when they are fwelled with the great rains. It is fometimes near a mile in breadth, having neither banks nor falls, but a very broad, flat bottom. When it is moft increafed, it has not, in the middle, above a fathom of water. During the greateft part of the year it is entirely dry. After running about twelve leagues from the lake of Chafcamuz, it enters into the River of Plata, a little above the Stony Point, or Punta de Piedra.

From

From this river to the Saladillo is about twelve leagues, travelling S. E. The intervening country is low and flat, like the reft; and in fome places there is plenty of pafture, efpecially on approaching nearer to the banks of the Saladillo. In dry feafons, when grafs fails near the coaft of the River of Plata, all the cattle belonging to the Spanifh farms of Buenos-Ayres are driven down to the banks of the Saladillo, where the grafs lafts longer, by reafon of the greater depth of foil.

Thefe plains extend to the weft as far as the Defaguadero, or territory of Mendoza, and have no water, but what falls from the fky, and is gathered in lakes, except the three rivers of the Defaguadero, Hueyguey, and Saladillo. This country is not inhabited or cultivated, either by Indians or Spaniards; but abounds with cattle, wild horfes, deer, oftriches, armadilloes, partridges, wild geefe, ducks, and other game.

The River Saladillo, on account of it's faltnefs, is only drinkable by cattle. Almoft all the year it runs fo low, that at a place called the Callighon, eight leagues from it's mouth, where it is very broad, it fcarce reaches to the ankles; and, even at it's mouth, it would be impoffible for a fmall boat laden to enter: yet, about the beginning of October, I have feen it fwell fo prodigioufly, as to rife to the tops of it's banks in four and twenty hours, and to have, in the place juft mentioned, near a fathom of water, and to be almoft a quarter of a mile in breadth; all this happening, without any quantity of rain having fallen in that part of the country. The flood generally lafts two or three months, before it goes down. The Saladillo breaks out where the Fifth River (that paffes by St. Louis) ends in a lake; which, when it overflows with the rains, or melted fnows, that fall

P

from

from the mountains, caufes the flooding of this river. As it takes it's courfe by the diftrict of Buenos-Ayres, going afterwards to the fouth, approaching the firft ridge of mountains, then turning to the north, and again to the eaft, it receives the waters of many vaft lakes, that overflow with the heavy rains; and, when thefe fupplies fail, it almoft dries up. On the banks of this river, to about eight leagues from the mouth, there are many woods, of a tree there called tala, which is only fit for fuel or enclofures. The laft of thefe woods, called the Ifla Larga, reaches to about three leagues from it's entrance into the River of Plata.

The River of Plata is one of the largeft rivers in all America, and opens into the fea by a mouth near feventy miles broad. Some fay it is only fixty, and others extend it to eighty. It is called by this name from the place where it joins with the Uruguaigh : higher up the principal branch, it goes by the name of the Parana. Into which enter the great rivers Bermejo, the Pilcomayu, which paffes by Chuquifaca, and the Paraguay (from whence that province takes it's name) which paffes by the city of Paraguay or Affumption, and communicates, by navigable branches, with the Portuguefe gold mines of Cuyaba and Matagroffo, as alfo with Peru; in the fame manner as the Parana communicates with the mines of Brafil and the mountains of St. Paul.

On the banks of the River Carcarania, or Tercero, about three or four leagues before it enters into the Parana, are found great numbers of bones, of an extraordinary bignefs, which feem human. There are fome greater and fome lefs, as if they were of perfons of different ages. I have feen thigh-bones, ribs, breaft-bones, and pieces of fkulls. I

have

have alfo feen teeth, and particularly fome grinders which were three inches in diameter at the bafe. Thefe bones (as I have been informed) are likewife found on the banks of the Rivers Parana and Paraguay, as likewife in Peru. The Indian Hiftorian, Garcilaffo de la Vega Inga, makes mention of thefe bones in Peru, and tells us that the Indians have a tradition, that giants formerly inhabited thofe countries, and were deftroyed by God for the crime of fodomy.

I myfelf found the fhell of an animal, compofed of little hexagonal bones, each bone an inch in diameter at leaft; and the fhell was near three yards over. It feemed in all refpects, except it's fize, to be the upper part of the fhell of the armadillo; which, in thefe times, is not above a fpan in breadth. Some of my companions found alfo, near the River Parana, an entire fkeleton of a monftrous alligator. I myfelf faw part of the vertebræ, each bone of which was near four inches thick, and about fix inches broad. Upon an anatomical furvey of the bones, I was pretty well affured, that this extraordinary increafe did not proceed from any acquifition of foreign matter; as I found that the bony fibres were bigger, in proportion as the bones were larger. The bafes of the teeth were entire, though the roots were worn away, and exactly refembled in figure the bafis of a human tooth, and not of that of any other animal I ever faw. Thefe things are well known to all who live in thefe countries; otherwife, I fhould not have dared to write them.

The River Parana has the extraordinary property of converting feveral fubftances into a very hard ftone.

When it was firft difcovered, it was navigable, by fmall fhips, as high as the City of the Affumption; but, fince that
time.

time, it has brought down so much sand, that even small merchant ships can go no higher than Buenos-Ayres. The larger vessels, and men of war, are obliged to unload at Montevideo. There is great need of good pilots for this river, to avoid foundering on the two banks, called the English Bank and the Bank of Ortiz, or striking against the Stony Point, which runs many leagues under the water, and crosses the whole river. The northern channel is narrower and deeper, the southern wider and more shallow: opposite to the bank of Ortiz it is not three fathom deep, with a hard stony bottom. This river has two annual inundations, a greater and a less, proceeding from the rains, which fall in those vast countries, from whence the Parana and Paraguay have their sources. The lesser is from the latter part of June to the latter part of July, is called the increase of the Pequereyes, or Sparlings, and is used to cover all the islands in the Parana. The greater begins in the month of December, and lasts all January, and sometimes February. This is so high, that it rises five or six yards above the islands, and sometimes more; so that there appears nothing above the water but the tops of the high trees, with which the islands of this river abound. In these seasons, the lions, tigers, stags, and aquaraquazues, leave the islands, and swim over to the main land. On an extraordinary and uncommon flood of this river, the inhabitants of Santa Fe have more than once had thoughts of forsaking the city, for fear of a deluge; but when this vast flood comes down into the River of Plata, it does but just cover the low lands upon it's banks.

Some of the islands of the Parana are two or three miles in length; they have great quantities of timber on them, and afford both food and shelter to great numbers of lions,

tigers,

tigers, ftags, capivaras, or river-hogs, river-wolves (which I take to be of the fame kind as our otter in England) aquaraquazues, and many alligators. The aquaraquazu is a very large fox, with a very bufhy tail; aquara (in the Paraguay tongue) fignifying fox, and quazu, great. Their common little fox they call aquarachay.

This river abounds in fifh of many kinds, both with and without fcales; fome of which are known, and others unknown in Europe. Thofe that have fcales, are the dorado or gold fifh, the packu, corvino, falmon, pequarey, lifa, boga, favala, dentudo, and other leffer fry. Thofe that have no fcales, are the mungrullu, zurubi, pati, armado, raya or ray, erizo or water hedge-hog, many river tortoifes, bagres, &c.

The dorado is in great plenty in moft of the rivers of the Parana. They are very large, fome weighing twenty or five and twenty pounds each; their flefh white and folid; the head in general moft efteemed.

The packu is the beft and moft delicious fifh of any in thefe rivers, and has an excellent tafte and flavour. It is a thick, broad fifh, like our turbot, of a dark, dufky colour, with a mixture of yellow. It's breadth is two thirds of it's length. It's fcales are very fmall, and the head is fmall in proportion to the body. This fifh is in high eftimation, and is feldom found but in the fpring and fummer. When falted with care, it may be kept fome months dried, but after that time, being very fat, it grows rancid. I think it is fomething like our tench, though much larger.

Another fifh, in great efteem, is the corvino; which is only found near the mouth of the River of Plata, where the falt and frefh water mix together. They are as large as a middle-fized cod, and in fhape refemble our carp. They

Q   have

have very large, thick bones, and broad fcales. This fifh is very good, either frefh, or falted and dried. At the proper feafon, great quantities of them are taken with a hook, about Maldonado and Montevideo, and are fent to Buenos-Ayres, Cordova, &c.

The falmon is not at all like ours, and is a dry, unfavoury fifh, in no efteem.

The pequareys, or king's fifh (fo called by the Spaniards) are a kind of fmelt or fparling; in colour, fhape, and tafte, refembling ours, except that the head is very large, and the mouth very wide. Their fize is about that of a mackerel. They never frequent falt water; but are in great quantities in the River of Plata. When the Parana increafes, in the month of July, they go up that river, in vaft fhoals, a little above Santa Fe, to leave their fpawn in the leffer rivers, which enter the Parana. The fifhermen catch them with hooks, in great quantities, cut them open, and dry them, and fell them to the neighbouring cities. They are of an excellent tafte, and their flefh is very white, without any fat: when frefh, they are confidered as a great dainty. They muft be dried without falt, as it would immediately confume them; and if they get any wet or moifture, where they are hung out to dry, they will corrupt. They are in equal efteem with the packu and the corvino.

The lifa, in fhape, fize, and tafte, refembles our mackerel; but is not of fo beautiful a colour, nor fo fmall near the tail, and the fcales are larger. This fifh fwims no higher than the River of Plata; where the greateft fhoals are to be found near the mouth, in the high tides. With the full and new moon, they enter in fuch numbers into the little River Saladillo, that in one night, in two or three draughts
with

with a drag-net, I generally made a fufficient provifion for myfelf and my companions during Lent.

The favala and boga are fifh like our carp. In the Parana, and River of Plata, they weigh three or four pounds. All the rivers of thefe provinces produce great quantities of thefe fifh, fo that they are very cheap; and the inhabitants lay in a great ftock of them, falted and dried. In eating of thefe fifh, great caution is requifite, on account of the multiplicity and fmallnefs of their bones. The boga, when frefh, is thought better than the favala, though that is both larger and broader. The method of taking them is with a net.

The dentudo (fo called on account of it's large and fharp fore-teeth) is fomewhat inferior to the laft. It may weigh in general about a pound and a half, and, though well-tafted, is feldom eaten, as it has great numbers of very dangerous bones. It is the moft thorny fifh I have ever feen.

There is, befides thefe, a fmall, broad, flat fifh, which is called palometa; it is thorny, but well-tafted. It has ugly, fharp fins, with which it wounds thofe, who too haftily lay hold of it. The wound which is made by thefe fins is very painful, fhoots, fefters, and inflames in fuch a manner, that it often brings on a fever, convulfions, and tetanus; fo that it fometimes terminates in death.

FISH without SCALES.

The mungrullu is the largeft fifh found in this river There are fome that weigh a hundred weight, and are two yards in length. It has a fmooth fkin, of an afh colour, fomewhat inclining to yellow, a bony head, rough gums, and a wide fwallow. The flefh is of a pale red, and very
folid.

folid. It is very ftrong and heavy in the water, and it requires very firm tackle, and great ftrength, to take it.

The zurubi is next in fize to the mungrullu, and not much inferior. It's head is almoft one third of it's whole bignefs, and is all bone. It has a very broad, flat mouth, and an exceeding wide throat. It's fkin is fmooth, of a white afh colour, fpotted like a tiger, with large, round, black fpots. It's flefh is white, found, folid, and well-tafted, and it is the beft of thefe fifh without fcales.

The pati, or patee, is not of a much lefs fize than the former, but has a fmaller head, and narrower fwallow, and has fome flefh upon the head. The colour of this fifh is like that of the mungrullu; it's flefh is of a yellowifh white; and it is efteemed almoft as much as the zurubi.

The armado is a thick, ftrong fifh, with a fhort body. It's back, fides, and fins, are all armed with ftrong, fharp points. When taken, it makes a grunting noife, and endeavours to wound; for which reafon it muft be ftunned, before it can be handled with fafety. This fifh generally weighs from about four to fix pounds; it's flefh is very white, firm, and folid.

The rayas, rays, or fkate, are fo very plentiful in the Parana, that the fhallow fandbanks are entirely covered with them. They are of an oval figure, near three quarters of a yard in length; the back is of a dark colour, and the belly white. They are flat, like ours, and have their mouth in the middle of the belly, which is indeed the greateft part of the fifh, the fkirts being very narrow, not above three inches broad, and much thinner than ours. As this is the only eatable part, they are in no efteem. This fifh has a long, narrow tail; at the root of which, on the back, it has a fharp, pointed bone, which has two

edges,

edges, rough like a faw with fmall teeth. With thefe, it wounds thofe who approach or tread upon it.

The wounds made by thefe bones are fometimes attended with very fatal confequences; for very frequently the bone is broken in the wound, and cannot be taken out, but by an incifion, very difficult to be performed in the tendinous parts of the feet. The wound becomes exceeding painful, inflames, does not fuppurate, brings on a fever with con vulfions, which ends in an ophifthotonos, or tetanus, and caufes death.

The erizo, or water hedge-hog, is very like the armado, but not quite fo large. Befides being armed in the fame manner, it has a very rough fkin, full of fhort, fharp points. It's flefh is not fo well-tafted as that of the armado.

The vieja, or old woman, bears a refemblance, both to the armado, and the erizo. It is armed with prickles, but they are neither fo ftrong, nor fo numerous, as thofe of the abovementioned fifh. It's fkin, which is of a motley grey colour, appears to be full of wrinkles; it grunts like the armado, when it is taken; and it's flefh is very favoury. Thefe feldom weigh two pounds, and, in the fmall brooks and rivers, they are ftill lefs, not weighing more than half a pound.

The bagres are in all refpects, except their fize, like the pati: they very feldom weigh fo much as a pound and a half, and oftentimes much lefs. They have a ftrong, pointed bone, in each of the fins near the head, and muft be handled with caution after they are taken, as they live a long time out of water. Their flefh is foft and well-tafted. They are either caught in nets, or by angling.

I fhall here give an account of a ftrange, amphibious animal, which is an inhabitant of the River Parana; a defcription of which has never reached Europe; nor is there even any mention made of it by thofe who have defcribed this country. What I here relate is from the concurrent affeverations of the Indians, and of many Spaniards who have been in various employments on this river. Befides, I myfelf, during my refidence on the banks of it, which was near four years, had once a tranfient view of one. So that there can be no doubt about the exiftence of fuch an animal.

In my firft voyage to cut timber, in the year 1752, up the Parana, being near the bank, the Indians fhouted yaquaru, and looking, I faw a great animal, at the time it plunged into the water from the bank; but the time was too fhort, to examine it with any degree of precifion.

It is called yaquaru, or yaquaruigh, which (in the language of that country) fignifies, the water tiger. It is defcribed by the Indians to be as big as an afs; of the figure of a large, over-grown river-wolf or otter; with fharp talons, and ftrong tufks; thick and fhort legs; long, fhaggy hair; with a long, tapering tail.

The Spaniards defcribe it fomewhat differently; as having a long head, a fharp nofe, like that of a wolf, and ftiff, erect ears. This difference of defcription may arife from it's being fo feldom feen, and, when feen, fo fuddenly difappearing; or perhaps there may be two fpecies of this animal. I look upon this laft account as the moft authentic, having received it from perfons of credit, who affured me they had feen this water tiger feveral times. It is always found near the river, lying on a bank; from whence, on hearing the leaft noife, it immediately plunges into the water.

It is very deftructive to the cattle which pafs the Parana; for great herds of them pafs every year; and it generally
happens

happens that this beast feizes fome of them. When it has once laid hold of it's prey, it is feen no more; and the lungs and entrails foon appear floating upon the water.

It lives in the greateft depths, efpecially in the whirlpools made by the concurrence of two ftreams, and fleeps in the deep caverns that are in the banks.

PORTS in the RIVER of PLATA.

The ports in this river, for fhips, are Buenos-Ayres, the Colony of the Sacrament, the Bay of Barragan, the Haven of Montevideo, and the Port of Maldonado. There are many others, for leffer veffels; chiefly at the mouths of the feveral rivers that run into it.

Buenos-Ayres (properly fpeaking) has no port, but only an open river, expofed to all the winds; and the more fo, becaufe the fhallownefs of the coaft obliges fhips to come to an anchor three leagues from the land. The winds here, efpecially thofe which come from the fouth, are very violent; and fhips are generally provided with cables and anchors of an uncommon ftrength, for this place.

The port of the Colony of the Sacrament is fomething better, by reafon of the covert it receives from the ifland of St. Gabriel and the higher land, and fhips being able to anchor near the fhore. Notwithftanding which, it is too open and expofed to the winds; and it has fome rocks and fhoals, and, in order to fteer into it with fafety, it is abfo-lutely neceffary to have a pilot.

The Bay of Barragan, which is twelve leagues to the fouth eaft of Buenos-Ayres, is likewife very wide and open, the land low all about it, nor can fhips of any burthen come within two or three leagues of the fhore. The only fhelter they have (if it may be fo called) are fome banks

under

under water, which break the force of the waves, but at the fame time are very inconvenient, both for going in and coming out; and there is but little fecurity, in a ftrong tempeft, againft a fhip's breaking her cable, and being driven on them.

Montevideo is the beft, and indeed the only good port, in this river. The Spaniards feem fenfible of the importance of this place, by the extraordinary care they have taken to fortify it; having made it much ftronger than Buenos-Ayres.

The entrance of this port is narrow, and through a ftrait made by two points of land. On that to the weft rifes a mountain, which may be feen at the diftance of twelve, or even fixteen leagues; from whence this place derives it's name. It is dangerous to fail too near the weftern point, as there are many rocks under water. The entrance to the eaft is deeper, and more fafe. Beyond the weftern point there is a fquare battery, built clofe to the water. When I faw it, it was only of ftone and clay, but fince, I believe, it has been rebuilt with lime. The bay, from the entrance, is more than a league and a half in length, and the bay itfelf is almoft round. Within it, on the eaft fide, there is a fmall ifland abounding with rabbits, called in Spanifh La Ifla de los Conejos. The furrounding land is fo very high, that no ftorm can reach this port (although there are very great ones in the river) the water being always as fmooth as that of a pool; and there is fufficient depth for fhips of the firft rate. I faw one of that fize here, which had formerly belonged to the States of Holland (and at that time belonged to the Marquis of Cafa Madrid) that had entered to unload. The bottom is a foft clay.

Behind the battery is the fmall city of Montevideo, which occupies all that part of a promontory, that forms the

eaftern

eaftern part of the bay. The fortifications are to the north. Thefe are regular works, according to the modern rules of military architecture; confifting of a line drawn from fea to fea, or from the bottom of the haven to the river, enclofing all the promontory; of a bulwark, or angle, in the middle, which faces the land-fide, and is well provided with artillery; and of a pretty ftrong fort, with barracks for foldiers, all bomb-proof. Towards the town, there is only a wall, with a ditch on both fides of it. This place has it's governor, and a garrifon of four or five hundred regular troops.

The other fide of the bay is without any fortification, nor has the high mountain even fo much as a watchtower; which mountain, if occupied, might be a great annoyance to the battery, city, and garrifon, on account of it's height, though it is four or five miles from the latter.

The laft port is Maldonado. It is an open haven, at the north entrance of the Plata, and is fheltered from the fouth eaft winds by a fmall ifland, which bears the fame name. Here the Spaniards have a fmall fort, where they keep a detachment of foldiers. I know no more of this port, having never feen it.

The northern fide of the River of Plata is an uneven country, has very high hills, and fome ridges of mountains. It is watered by a great many brooks and rivers; fome of which laft are very large. The biggeft of thefe are the rivers St. Lucie, the Uruguaigh, and the Rio Negro, which falls into the Uruguaigh, about ten leagues from it's mouth. This country is very fertile, produces all kinds of grain, when properly cultivated, and has alfo great quantities of good timber. The rivers and brooks are all of frefh water. Here are a great many farms belonging to the Spaniards; but the

S

country

country to the north of Montevideo is poffeffed by the infidel Minuanies.

The Charonas and Garoes (two of thefe nations) were formerly very numerous, but have been entirely deftroyed by the Spaniards. In this territory, there were formerly the greateft numbers both of wild and tame cattle; and here they increafe more than on the fouthern fide of the River of Plata. There are ftill great numbers of fheep and horned cattle, but few horfes. A great quantity of contrayerva grows in the neighbourhood of Montevideo; which is capable of all the products of Europe.

The Spanifh territory is bounded on the north by the Rio Grande, which divides it from the Portuguefe fettlements in the Brafils.

CHAPTER III.

Continuation of the Defcription of the Indian Country, with it's Vales, Mountains, Rivers, &c.—Terra del Fuego.—Falkland's Iflands.

TO the fouth of the town of the Conception (which is upon the fouth fide of the River of Plata) is the mount of the Vivoras, or Vipers; where are two thick woods, almoft round, with a fpace between them. About four leagues to the fouth of thefe is the Mónte del Tordillo, or of the Grey Horfe, which confifts of a great number of woods, fome greater and fome lefs, each of them fituated on a rifing ground encompaffed with a vale; their trees the fame as thofe of the woods on the

Saladillo.

Saladillo. All this is a plain, low country, with high watery grafs, and abounds in armadilloes, deer, oftriches, and wild horfes; and in the woods there are both lions and tigers. Some parts of thefe woods reach within two leagues of the feacoaft, which is extremely low, and fo boggy that it is im-paffable, the boggy part being near a mile in breadth, and ex-ceedingly deep.

All the way from the Saladillo to near the firft mountains there is neither brook nor river, nor any water but what is collected in the lakes in rainy feafons; and in times of drought even thefe fail.

About fifteen or twenty leagues to the E. S. E. or E. by S. of the woods of the Tordillo is the great promontory of Cape St. Anthony, which forms the fouthern point of the River of Plata. The figure of this cape is round, and not pointed, as is reprefented in fome maps. It ftands in a peninfula; the entrance into which on the weftern fide is over a wide boggy brook, or lake, which comes from the fea, or the falt water of the River of Plata. It is chiefly a clay, with fome little depth of foil, and is watered in winter by many fmall brooks, whofe waters have a falt tafte; but they are generally dry in fummer. The paftures are not fo good, nor the grafs fo high, as thofe of the Tordillo and the Saladillo. On the fouth fide of the promontory an arm of the weftern ocean enters, forms a bay, and terminates in lakes. Whether this bay might ferve as a harbour is not known, as it has never been founded; all fhips fteering very wide of the Cape, for fear of the great fand-banks called Arenas Gordas, or Thick Sands. I have been round fome part of thefe lakes, and paffed the channels by which others have a communication with the bay; but with great danger, not only from the bogs, but more efpecially from the tigers,

which

which were more numerous than I ever faw in any other place. Upon the borders of thefe lakes there are very thick woods of tala and elder trees, which are the retreats of thefe fierce animals, whofe chief food is fifh.

Towards the coaft, there are three ridges of fand. That which is neareft the fea is very high and loofe, and moves with the winds: at a diftance it has the appearance of a mountain. The next is about half a mile diftant from the former, and is not fo high. The third is ftill at a greater diftance, extremely low and narrow, the fand here being fcarcely two feet high. The land between thefe ridges of fand is barren, being almoft deftitute of herbage of any kind. This peninfula abounds with wild horfes, which (it is imagined) having got in from the neighbouring country, could not find their way out again; which circumftance oc- cafions it to be a frequent refort of the Indian hunters. This fmall territory is called by the Spaniards the Rincon (or cor- ner) of Tuyu, the country adjoining being called Tuyu, for more than forty leagues to the weft. Tuyu in the Indian language fignifies mire or clay, which is the foil of all that country, and continues fouthward to within ten leagues of the firft mountains. The ridges of fand abovementioned reach fouth to within three leagues of Cape Lobos, having to the weft of them low, boggy marfhes, of two leagues or more in breadth, which extend all along the coaft, before you come to the higher ground of the Tuyu, which begins at no great diftance from the woods of the Tordillo. In this country there are a great many little hills, which run eaft and weft, and about two or three leagues from each other. They are ufually double; and at the foot of each of them is a lake, of one, two, and fometimes three miles in length: the moft remarkable of which lakes are the Bravo, the

Palantalen,

Palantalen, Lobos, Cerrillos, &c. Thefe hills form in general high banks towards the lakes; which, without having any brook, river, or fpring to fupply them, feldom want water, except in times of great drought. They are called by the Spaniards Cerrillos (or little hills) and there are fome of them even on the other fide of the Saladillo.

This country, during fome parts of the year, fwarms with incredible numbers of wild horfes; and on this account the Tehuelhets, Chechehets, and fometimes all the tribes of the Puelches and Moluches affemble here, to get their ftock of provifions. They difperfe their little moveable habitations upon the fmall hills beforementioned. and hunt every day till they have taken what is fufficient, and then return to their refpective countries.

Near the fea-fide, and almoft clofe to the great ridges of fand, is a great lake, called the Mar Chiquito, or Little Sea. It is about five leagues diftant from Cape Lobos, and is about the fame number of leagues in length, though not above two or three miles broad. It is falt, and communicates with the ocean by a river which paffes through the fand-banks. There are alfo three or four fmall rivers, that iffue from the north fide of the mountains of the Vuulcan and Tandil, and croffing the plain from weft to eaft, occafion fome bogs or marfhes, and empty themfelves into this lake. Thefe rivers are of fweet water, and have fome bagres in them, with great numbers of otters, as before defcribed: the largeft of them is that which comes from the Tandil, and enters into the northern point of the lake.

To the north of thefe rivers the foil grows confiderably better, the grafs being high and verdant, and fo continuing to the foot of the mountains; but there are no woods, nor

T

even

even fingle trees. The mountains, though they are not very high, may be diftinguifhed very plainly in a clear day at the diftance of twenty leagues, the country being fo extremely flat and level.

Thefe mountains are not one continued ridge, but many mountains or ridges of mountains, and between them are large, pleafant vales, which interrupt their continuation. They begin to rife at about fix leagues diftance from the fea-coaft, and continue for about forty leagues to the weft. They rife from the plain almoft perpendicular, and are covered with grafs till within about ten yards of the top; and from thence there are great numbers of ftones, which lie in fuch a manner as to form a wall, that enclofes the mountain, except at one end, where it declines gradually. The declining part is divided into hills and dales, with fmall rivulets, which join at the bottom, and form one common ftream. At the top there is a large country, with variety of rocks, hollows, and hills; with deep brooks, running among frequent breaks of the leffer hills: there are alfo fmall woods of a low, thorny tree, very fit for fuel. This variety of country is from two to three leagues in length, and fome-times a league in breadth, fometimes more, efpecially at that end where it declines. At the foot of thefe mountains there are abundance of fprings, which trickle down into the vallies and form brooks. The paths by which they are afcended are very few, and extremely narrow. Thefe the Indians ftop up, to fecure the wild horfes, &c. taken in the Tuyu, which they turn upon the top, as there is no getting from thence but by thefe narrow paffes, which are eafily ftopped.

Between thefe mountains there is a fpace, about two or three leagues broad, of a plain level country, with fome

few

few rifing grounds, watered with brooks; which fometimes run in the middle, and fometimes round them, and are formed by the fprings which iffue from the mountains. Thefe vallies are very fertile, have a deep, black foil, without any clay, and are always covered with fuch fine grafs, that the cattle which feed there grow fat in a very fhort time. They are in general very much enclofed by the mountains at one end, or by fome high hill which rifes in the middle; are moft commonly open to the north or north weft; and from the rifing ground there is a pleafant and delightful profpect a great way into the country, all the enclofed vales between the mountains being higher land than the plains to the north. I have not feen any country, in the diftrict of Buenos-Ayres, fo capable of improvement as this. The only inconvenience it is fubject to is the want of good timber for building houfes; which however, in the courfe of a few years, and with fome little trouble, might be remedied; efpecially as there are fufficient materials for temporary houfes, with roofs covered with reeds, which might ferve till better could be had.

The fmall rivulets, or brooks, that flow from the mountains, fometimes enter into, or form lakes; fome of which are more than a league in length. There is one of an oval figure, that reaches from mountain to mountain, and is in windy feafons very boifterous. There is alfo another, called the Lake of the Cabrillos, which is in the fhape of the figure 7, and is as long, but not fo broad as the former. On this lake there are great quantities of ducks, of various kinds and colours, fome of them as large as geefe; and on one point of it I faw fuch numbers, that it was a difficult matter to difcern the water, though wide. On one fide of this lake there are hills, and, on the other, a high, broken bank. At one

point

point there enters a fmall river, that comes from the mountains, and, having no immediate drain or channel to carry it
off, breaks out, after running under ground, at the diftance
of a league, between the lake and the feacoaft.

That part of the mountains which falls to the eaft, and is
neareft to the fea, is called by the Spaniards Vulcan, from a
miftake or corruption of the Indian name, Vuulcan, or
Voolcan; there being a large opening to the fouth, and
Vuulcan, in the Moluche tongue, fignifying an opening.
Volcanoes there are none; though the Spanifh word feems
to imply that there are fuch in this country. The middle
part is called Tandil, or (as we pronounce it) Tandeel, from
a mountain of that name, which is higher than the reft.
The laft point of this ridge of mountains towards the weft is
called the Cayru.

To the eaft of the Vuulcan, towards the fea, the country
is unequal for about two leagues; after which it is flat, with
brooks and watering places. Here are fome thick and almoft
impenetrable woods, as well in the hilly as in the low country;
in which are a great deal of the low, thorny tree, that grows
on the mountains, and plenty of elder trees, which here
grow very thick, and to the height of fix or feven yards.
The fruit is like ours, but very good to eat, being of a four
tafte corrected with an agreeable fweetnefs. In other countries, to the north, as Buenos-Ayres, Cordova, &c. the fruit
is of a bitter, naufeous tafte, and the tree does not grow fo
high. Near the feacoaft, about three miles diftant from the
fea, is a rifing ground, which continues along the coaft for
about four leagues, and is exceedingly fertile, with rich
paftures, where the cattle become extremely fat.

Near the fhore, in this part, are two little, round hills,
called the Cerros de los Lobos, or Hills of the Sea-Wolves.

The

The shore itself consists of high rocks and large stones. Here are great herds of sea-wolves and sea-lions (such as are described in Lord Anson's Voyage) who sleep on the rocks, and suckle their young in the great caves in them. In the woods there are many lions, but few tigers.

Lower towards the south, the coast for many leagues, as far as the mouth of the Red River, or the First Desaguadero, has perpendicular banks, of such a vast height, that it is frightful to approach the brink of them; but these terminate in low sands and sand-banks. All along this coast there are many small brooks and rivers, which, crossing the plains from the beforementioned mountains, enter into the ocean.

The country between the first mountains and the Cafuhati is plain and open, and the Indians are commonly four days in passing it, when they travel without tents. The Chechehets, who travel to the Red River, go straight from the Vuulcan, nearer to the coast, and pass between the Cafuhati and the sea, about fifteen leagues to the east of that mountain, and as much from the sea to the west; that they may avoid a vast, sandy desart, called Huecuvu Mapu, or the Devil's Country; where they and their families might be overwhelmed, if a wind should arise at the time they are passing over it.

The Cafuhati is the beginning of a great chain of mountains, which forms a kind of triangle, whereof this makes one angle; and from hence one side of the triangle extends to the Cordillera of Chili, and another terminates in the Straits of Magellan; yet not without being sometimes interrupted by vallies, and continued chains of mountains, that run from north to south, with many windings. That part which forms the Cafuhati is by much the highest. In the centre of some lower hills rises a very lofty mountain, that is as high as the Cordillera, and is always covered with snow;

U   and

and it is very feldom that any Indian ventures to the top of it. From this high mountain all this part derives it's name; Cafu in the Puel tongue, denoting hill or mountain, and Hati, or Hatee, high. The Moluches call it Vuta Calel, or Great Bulk. Some brooks and ftreams break out from the fouthern part of this mountain, that have deep banks covered with willows, which ferve for enclofures to fecure the cattle of the Indians. After running more to the fouth, they join and form a fmall river, which, running fouth eaft, enters into the Hueyque Leuvu, or Little River of Sauces, at fome diftance from it's mouth. The hills of the Cafuhati, after continuing about three or four leagues to the weft, have an opening of about three hundred yards wide, which they who take this rout (and not that between the Cafuhati and the Red River) are obliged to pafs. It is called the Guamini, or Guaminee, and has on both fides of it very fteep hills. All the country near thefe hills is open and pleafant, and abounding in paftures. The good enclofures that the hills and brooks afford for the cattle, and the plains to the weftward having plenty of game, occafion it to be conftantly inhabited by Indians of different nations; who fucceed each other according to their ftrength, the weakeft being always obliged to leave the place.

To the weftward of the vaft country of the Tuyu, down to the woods which are over againft the Cafuhati, is the country of the Dihuihets; having thefe woods to the fouth, the Taluhets and jurifdiction of Cordova to the north, and the Pehuenches to the weft. That part of this country which falls to the eaftward is open and champaign, with very few woods or coppices, but is fubject to frequent inundations in fome parts, from the great fall of rains and the overflowing of many extenfive lakes. Some of thefe, which lie to the

weft

weſt and the ſouth of this country, produce as fine a cryſtal-line-grained ſalt as thoſe of St. Lucar. The Spaniards of Buenos-Ayres take a journey every year to theſe lakes, with a guard of ſoldiers, to defend them and their cattle from the attacks of the Indians, and load two or three hundred carts with this neceſſary commodity. The diſtance from Buenos-Ayres to theſe ſalt lakes is about one hundred and fifty leagues. They are very large and broad, and ſome of them encompaſſed with wood to a conſiderable diſtance. Their banks are white with the ſalt; which needs no other preparation, than being a little expoſed to the ſun and dried.

Farther to the weſtward there is a river with very high, ſteep banks; whence it is called by the Spaniards Rio de las Barancas, or River of Banks. It is called by the Indians Hueyque Leuvu, or River of Sauces, or Willows, which grow on it's banks. This river is of a conſiderable ſize, though little when compared with the Red River and the Black River. It is in general ſhallow, and may be waded, but has ſometimes great floods, from rains and melted ſnows. It is formed in the plain country between the mountains of Achala, Yacanto, and the Firſt Deſaguadero, or Red River, from a great number of brooks which iſſue from thoſe mountains, and takes it's courſe from thence ſouth and ſouth eaſt, till it paſſes within twelve or fourteen leagues to the eaſt of the Caſuhati, and enters into the ocean, after having received another ſmall river which flows from that mountain. But I have ſome doubts, from the relations of the Indians, that this river does not empty itſelf immediately into the ocean, but into the Red River, a little above it's mouth. All this country abounds with wild horſes, eſpecially the eaſtern part, that lies neareſt to the Tuyu and the mountains.

The country between the Hueyque Leuvu and the Red
River

River is much the fame, but rather more abounding in lakes and marfhes intermixed with woods.

The Firft Defaguadero, or Red River, is one of the largeft that pafs through this country. It takes it's rife from a great number of ftreams that break forth from the weftern fide of the Cordillera, almoft as high as Chuapa, the moft northern town of Chili; and, taking an almoft direct courfe from north to fouth, abforbs all the rivers which flow from this fide of the Cordillera, befides a vaft quantity of melted fnow. It paffes, with a deep and rapid current, within about ten leagues of San Juan and Mendoza: near the latter of which places it receives the great river Tunuya, and another called the River of Portillio, that joins with it, and is foon after fwallowed up in the lakes of Guanacache.

Thefe lakes are famous for the great numbers of trout caught in them, but more fo for burying as it were in their bofom fo vaft a river; becaufe here it feems to end, terminating in brooks and marfhes. But at a few leagues diftance it breaks out again, in a vaft number of rivulets, which, joining together, form one common river, called by the Picunches, Huaranca Leuvu, that is, a Thoufand Rivers; either from the many leffer rivers of which it is compofed, or it's great breadth; it being after this very broad and fhallow till it enters the ocean. The Pehuenches call this river Cum Leuvu, or Red River, it's banks being of a red colour.

In the winter, when the ground is hardened by the frofts, the Indians, &c. pafs over the marfhes without any inconvenience; but when, by the heat of the fun, the fnow melts in the Cordillera, the Defaguadero increafes to fuch a degree, that it overflows the lakes and marfhes, and renders them, as well as the Red River impaffable, except by thofe

who

who are dexterous fwimmers: an ability the Pehuenches and Picunches have not.

This river, from the part where the little rivers join it, directs it's courfe to the fouth eaft, till it approaches within a day's journey of the Second Defaguadero, or Black River; when it turns due eaft for about fifty leagues, approaching the Cafuhati: it then turns again to the fouth eaft; in which courfe it continues till it difcharges itfelf into the fea. The mouth of this river makes a large bay or opening, but is very fhallow, being ftopped up with mud and fand banks.

Sometime in this century a Spanifh veffel was loft at the mouth of this river, in the Bahia Anegada; the crew of which faved themfelves in one of the boats, and failing up the river, arrived at Mendoza. In the year 1734, or there-abouts, the mafts and part of the hulk remained, and were feen by the Spaniards, who at that time made an incurfion within land, with their field-marfhal Don Juan de Samartin, who told it me as an eye-witnefs. The courfe of this river therefore is eftablifhed paft all doubt.

The Tehuelhets of the Black River, and the Huilliches, in their journey to the Cafuhati, pafs this river in the two places where it takes thefe turns or windings to the eaft and fouth eaft. It may be near a hundred and fifty yards wide in thefe places, but not fo deep but that it may be waded, except when it is raifed by the rains and melted fnows. It is then fo deep, that the women and tents cannot pafs, and only the men who can fwim, with their horfes. The Chechehets, in their journey betwixt their own and the Spanifh territories, pafs it near the mouth.

The country which lies between this river and the River Sanquel (which difcharges itfelf into the Second Defagua-dero) is full of marfhes, and woods of that thorny, thick,

X   rough

rough reed, that is called Sanquel in the idiom of the Pehuenches; so as to be impaffable in any other manner, than
by going clofe to the Cordillera, and paffing the river at it's
fource, or where it iffues from thofe mountains.

Twelve leagues to the weft of the Cafuhati, and about fix
or eight from the Guamini, the Hueyque Leuvu before-
mentioned takes it's courfe. The way to this river confifts of
hills, dales, ftony mountains, and many woods. Thefe
woods are fo extremely thick, that they are paffable only
through two ftrait paths, which lead to the River Colorado,
or Red River: one points to the weft, and the other inclines
to the fouth. Thefe woods continue above twenty leagues
to the north of the Colorado; to the fouth, they extend to
the Second Defaguadero, but there they are fomewhat
thinner; and, to the weft, they reach to the River Sanquel:
after which their thicknefs diminifhes. At about five or fix
leagues to the weftward of the River Hueyque there is a
large falt pond, in the middle of the woods, and about five
or fix leagues farther there is a fecond. There are likewife
two others; one to the fouth, and another to the north.
They are well ftored with an excellent clean falt, of which
the Indians provide themfelves great quantities in their
journeys. There is alfo another very large falt pond not far
from the fea coaft, between the Firft and Second Defaguadero.

From the River Hueyque to the Firft Defaguadero, or
Red River, is four, and fometimes five days journey, with
tents; which, at that part where it bends towards the fouth,
is through thick, low woods. From thence, travelling ftill
to the weft, upon the bank of this river, with the woods to
the north, for five or fix days more, you arrive at the place
where it comes from the north and doubles to the eaft; and
here

here it is paffed : when, after a long day's journey, directly
to the fouth, over a craggy country encumbered with woods,
where is no place to reft, the Black River, or Second
Defaguadero, is feen from the hills, which are very high,
running in a deep, broad vale, which is about two leagues
in breadth on each fide of the river.

This river, the greateft of all Patagonia, empties itfelf into
the weftern ocean, and is known by various names ; as the
Second Defaguadero, or Second Drain ; the Defaguadero of
Nahuelhuaupi, or Drain of Nahuelhuaupi ; by the Spa-
niards called the Great River of Sauces, or Willows ; by
fome of the Indians, Cholehechel ; by the Puelches, Leuvu
Camo, or the River, by Antonomafia ; and Cufu Leuvu,
that is, Rio Negro, or Black River, by the Huilliches and
Pehuenches. Where they crofs from the Firft to the Second
Defaguadero, it is called Cholehechel.

The real fource of this river is not exactly known, but it is
fuppofed to rife not far from the beginnings of the River Sanquel. It is formed by a great many brooks and fmall rivers,
runs unfeen among high, broken rocks, and is ftraitened
and locked up in a very narrow and deep channel ; till at
length it begins to fhow itfelf in a very wide, deep, and rapid ftream, fomewhat higher than Valdivia, but on the oppofite fide of the Cordillera. At a fmall diftance from it's firft
appearance many rivers fall into it ; fome of which are large,
and come from the Cordillera, and enter principally on the
north fide.

A Tehuel or Southern Cacique defcribed upon my table
as many as fixteen, and told me their names, but not having
writing materials at hand, I could not fet them down, and
have fince forgotten them. He added likewife, that he knew
no place in the river, even before the entry of thefe leffer
ones,

ones, that was not very wide and deep. He did not know where it began, but said it came from the north. He was brother to the old Cacique Cacapol, appeared to be upwards of seventy years of age, and had lived all his time on the borders of this river.

Of these rivers which enter on the north side, one is large, broad, and deep, and proceeds from a vast lake, near twelve leagues in length, and almost round, called Huechun Lavquen, or the Lake of the Boundary. This lake is about two days journey from Valdivia, and is formed by several brooks, springs, and rivers, which come from the Cordillera.

Besides the river it sends forth to the east and south, which makes part of the great river, it may send out another westward, which may communicate with the South Sea near Valdivia: but this I cannot affirm, as I did not sufficiently examine it.

There is also from the north another small river, which comes higher up from the foot of the Cordillera, and crosses the country from N. W. to S. E. This falls into the Desaguadero about a day and a half's journey to the east of Huichin, the country of the Cacique Cangapol. It is called Pichee Picuntu Leuvu, that is, the Little Northern River; to distinguish it from the Sanquel, which also enters into the Second Desaguadero; each of them being called by the Indians the River of the North. The mouth of this river is distant from that of the Sanquel about four or five days march.

The river Sanquel is one of the largest in this country, and may pass for another Desaguadero, or Drain, of the snowy mountains of the Cordillera. It comes very far north, running between the mountains amongst deep breaks and pre-

cipices,

cipices, all the way augmented with new supplies from the many brooks that join it. It's first appearance is at a place called the Diamante, or Diamond; from whence it is called by the Spaniards Rio del Diamante. At a small distance from it's source considerable brooks enter it, that come from the foot of the Cordillera farther north; and lower down, towards the south, the River Lolgen discharges itself into it. This river is so large, that the main stream, by the Indians of the Black River, is indifferently called Sanquel Leuvu and Lolgen. It is broad and rapid even at it's first appearance, and increases by the many brooks and springs it receives from the mountains, and from the very moist country through which it passes for the space of three hundred miles, taking an almost straight course from N. to S. by E. till it enters into the Second Desaguadero, or Black River, by a very wide and open mouth.

At the conflux of these two rivers there is a great whirl-pool; yet in this very place the Indians pass it, swimming over with their horses. The current of the Sanquel throughout is very violent, especially on it's increase. It's banks are covered with reeds and very lofty willows.

On the south side of the Great or Second Desaguadero there enter but two rivers of any note. One is called the Lime Leuvu by the Indians, and by the Spaniards the Desaguadero, or Drain, of Nahuelhuaupi, or Nauwelwapi. The people of Chili give the same name to all the great river; but this is through a mistake, they being ignorant of some of it's branches; of which this is only one, and not so big as the Sanquel, and much less than the main branch, even at it's first appearance out of the Cordillera.

This river proceeds, with a great and rapid stream, from the Lake of Nahuelhuaupi, almost due north, through vales

and

and marshes, and continues it's course for about thirty leagues, receiving a great many brooks in it's passage from the neighbouring hills, till it enters into the Second Desaguadero, something lower than that which comes from Huechun Lavquen, or the Lake of the Boundary. It is called by the Indians Lime Leuvu, because the vales and marshes through which it flows abound with ticks and blood-leeches, and these are called in the tongue of the Huilliches, lime, or leeme; and the country Leeme Mapu, the Country of Ticks; and the people Leeme Che, People of Ticks.

The Lake of Nahuelhuaupi is one of the greatest that is formed by the waters of the Cordillera, and (according to the account of the Chilenian Missionaries) is near fifteen leagues in length. On one side of it, near it's bank, is a small, low island, called Nahuelhuaupi, or the Island of Tigers; nahuel signifying a tiger, and huaupi an island. It is situated in a great plain, encompassed by hills, rocks, and mountains; from which it receives many brooks and springs, as well as water from the melted snows. A small river enters it on the south side, which comes from the country of Chonos, on the continent over against Chiloe.

The other river which enters the Second Desaguadero from the south is but small, and is called by the Indians Machi Leuvu, or the River of Wizards; but wherefore, I know not. It comes from the country of the Huilliches, runs from south to north, and discharges itself into the main river a little lower than the Lime Leuvu.

The Second Desaguadero from hence takes it's course to the east, making a small bend northward as it comes to the Cholehechel, where it approaches within ten or twelve leagues of the First Desaguadero; then it winds downward to the south east, till it enters into the ocean.

Some

Some small distance below this last winding it makes a large sweep, or circle, forming a peninsula; the neck of it is about three miles wide, and the peninsula, which is almost round, is about six leagues over. It is called the Enclosure of the Tehuelhets, or Tehuel-Malal. The river, till it comes to this enclosure, has high hills and mountains on both sides, but so far distant, as to leave, in many places, plains between them and the river of two or three miles broad, which abound with pasture for cattle, and are never sown: In other places the hills come close to the water. The banks are covered with willows, and it contains a few islands dispersed here and there; among which there is one of a large size, in the country of the Cacique Cacapol, where that chief and his vassals secure their horses from being stolen by the Pehuenches. I never heard of any falls in this river, or that it is fordable in any part of it. It is very rapid, and the floods are very extraordinary, when the rains and melted snows come down the west side of the Cordillera, comprehending all that falls from thirty-five to forty-four degrees of southern latitude, being a chain of seven hundred and twenty miles of mountains. This rising of the river is so sudden, that though it may be heard at a great distance, beating and roaring among the rocks, yet it hardly gives sufficient notice to the Indian women, to pull down their tents, and carry off their baggage; nor to the Indian men, to secure their cattle by removing them to the mountains. Many disasters happen oftentimes in consequence of this great flood; the whole vale is deluged, and tents, cattle, and sometimes women and children, are carried down the vast, impetuous torrent.

The mouth of this river, which opens into the Atlantic Ocean, has, I believe, never been properly surveyed. It is called the Bay Sans Fond, or Bottomless Bay; whether from

it's

it's depth, or it's fhallownefs (as fome imagine) I do not know, but I fhould rather imagine from the former; for I cannot fuppofe that a river fo extremely rapid, and which takes a courfe of near three hundred leagues, from the foot of the Cordillera, among rocks and ftones, could carry along with it any great quantity of fand; or, if it did, that the fand could lodge at the mouth, againft the force of fo violent a current. The Spaniards call it the Bay of Saint Matthias, and place it in forty degrees forty-two minutes fouth latitude; though in Mr. D'Anville's map it is placed two degrees farther from the line. I cannot think the diftance is fo great between the Firft and Second Defaguaderoes; all the Indians affirming that thefe two rivers enter into the fea at no great diftance from each other: wherefore, in my map, I have taken a middle diftance.

In an expedition in the year 1746, to examine the fea-coaft, &c. between the River of Plata and the Straits of Magellan, the mouth of this river was not examined, although the captain of the fhip was urged to make the proper difpofitions for fuch an examination; but he neglected to give notice when he was got near to it's latitude. His reafons for this conduct were, " that his orders were only to difcover if " there was any port, fit to make a fettlement, near or not " very far from the mouth of the Straits, that might afford " fupplies for fhips in their paffage to the South Seas; that " he had furveyed all from Port Gallegos, without finding " one place fit for forming a fettlement upon, on account of " the barrennefs of the foil, and the want of the common " neceffaries of wood and water; that he had done what was " fufficient to quiet the King of Spain, with refpect to any " jealoufies he might have of a certain northern nation's being " fo foolifh as to attempt a fettlement in fuch a country,

" where

" where as many as were left muft perifh; that the Bay Sans
" Fond was at too great a diftance from Cape Horn, to
" come within the circle of his inftructions; that his ftock
" of frefh water was fcarce fufficient to reach the River of
" Plata, and that he was not certain whether he fhould be
" able to get any more at the mouth of the River of Sauces."

A fettlement at the mouth of this river would be much
more convenient for fhips going to the South Seas than that
of Buenos-Ayres; where a fhip may be a fortnight, or a
month, before it can get out, on account of the contrary
winds, and then not being able to get over the flats but at
high water: and after this, it will take up a week, to get
down as low as the Bay Sans Fond; when a veffel that failed
from hence might by that time have doubled Cape Horn,
and got into the South Sea.

If any nation fhould think proper to people this country,
it might be the caufe of perpetual alarm to the Spaniards; as
from hence fhips might be fent into the South Seas, and their
fea ports deftroyed, before fuch a fcheme or intention could
be known in Spain, or even in Buenos-Ayres. And farther,
a nearer way might be difcovered, by navigating the river
with barges near to Valdivia. Many troops of the Indians
of the river, the ftouteft of all thefe nations, would enlift
themfelves for the fake of plunder; fo that the important
garrifon of Valdivia might be eafily taken; which would of
courfe draw after it the taking of Valparaifo, a much weaker
fortrefs; and the poffeffion of thefe two places would enfure
the conqueft of the fertile kingdom of Chili.

A fettlement is much more practicable here, than in the
Malouin Iflands, or the Ports of Defire and San Julian;
here being plenty of wood and water, and a good country,
fit for tillage, and able to maintain it's inhabitants. The con-

Z   veniences

veniences for a settlement on the enclosure of the Tehuelhets are very great; it being defended by this great and rapid
river, which forms as it were a natural foss, and containing
eighteen miles in length of a very fruitful country, abounding with pastures, and stored with plenty of hares, rabbits,
wild fowl, deer, &c. and from the river it might be supplied
with plenty of fish of various kinds.

It is a consideration of some weight, that the settlers
might be provided with cattle, as cows, horses, &c. on
the spot, at a very trifling expense. A commerce might also
be established with the Indians; who for sky-coloured glass
beads, cascabells of cast brass, broad swords, heads of lances,
and hatchets, would exchange cattle for the use of the colony, and fine furs to send to Europe. And so rare is it that
ships meet in these seas, that all this might be done with so
much secrecy, that the place might be peopled and main-
tained many years, without the Spaniards being informed of
it. The French, for instance, were settled several years in
those southern islands, without it's being known to the nations of Europe.

The woods hereabouts consist of the same kind of trees
as are before described, except one sort, which the Indians regard as sacred, and never burn. It produces a gum, of the
consistence, and almost of the colour of yellow wax: on
burning, it has a very fragrant smell, but is not like any of
the officinal gums used among us. I never saw this tree; but
the natives informed me it is but small. I have had some
small quantities of the gum, which, mixed with wax, made
small candles.

All the seacoast, from about twenty leagues to the south
of the Second Desaguadero, is a dry, barren country, with
very little pasture, and uninhabited by man or beast, except
a few

a few guanacoes, that fometimes defcend from the neighbour-ing mountains to the weft. It has no water for a great part of the year, and what it has is to be found only in the lakes after great rains. At that feafon the Indians come down to this country, to bury their dead, and vifit the fepulchres, and to feek for falt at St. Julian's Bay, or upon the feacoaft. Some few ftony hills are difperfed here and there, and a me-tallic ore, of a fpecies of copper, was found in fome of them, at Port Defire.

In the voyage made in 1746, no river was difcovered in all this coaft, though every where (efpecially in the ports de-fcribed in the old maps) the Spaniards and miffionaries went afhore, and travelled all round the different ports. This convinced them of the miftake they had been under; which was probably occafioned by the ftrong eddies, or running out of the water at the low tides. As for the River Camarones, defcribed in Mr. D'Anville's map, as opening at the bottom of the Bay of St. George with three mouths (and not in the Bay of Camarones, as I have feen it in former maps) I have placed it in my map, upon his authority; but at the fame time muft obferve, that in the abovementioned voyage no fuch river was difcovered, though we entered into this wide bay. The diftance perhaps which the fhip lay from the fhore might be too great for our making certain ob-fervations. The Indians indeed fpeak of a river in the country of Chulilaw; but I could not difcover whence it came, or where it ended, or whether, being fmall, it was not fwallowed up in thofe defarts; as it often happens to other greater rivers defcribed in this map.

In the Bay of Lions the Spaniards went afhore, but did not find any river. In the Bay of Camarones there was nothing remarkable, but many huge rocks, that had the ap-

pearance

pearance of a city under water. The bottom of this bay was fo fhallow at low water, that the frigate was left upon the rocks, and was obliged to wait for the tide to get off. In the Gallegos Bay they likewife went afhore, but were called on board again, before a thorough inquiry could be made whether there was a river or not.

The territory of the Tehuelhet and other Patagonian nations borders upon the weftern parts of this uninhabitable country; and according to the relation of fome Spanifh captives, whom I refcued from flavery among the Indians (one of them had been feven years in that country) all this part confifts of vales enclofed within low ridges of mountains, watered with fprings and fmall brooks, which are fwallowed up in little lakes, or watering places, that in fummer dry up: fo that many of the inhabitants, at that feafon, go to live on the Second Defaguadero, carrying their wives, families, and all their baggage along with them; and fome go even as far as the Cafuhati, the Vuulcan, and the Tandil.

Thefe vales abound in paftures, and have fome fmall woods, which ferve for fuel. There are plenty of guanacoes in this country, and in fome places they make their tents of the fkins of this animal. There are likewife great numbers of antas, whofe fkins the Tehuelhets fell to the other Puelches, with which the latter make their armour.

The anta is of the ftag kind, but without horns. It's body is as big as that of a large afs; it's head very long and tapering, ending in a fmall fnout; it's body very ftrong, and broad at the fhoulders and haunches; it's legs and fhanks are long, and ftronger than thofe of a ftag; it's feet cloven like thofe of a ftag, but fomething larger; it's tail fhort, like that of a deer. The ftrength of this animal is wonderful; it being able to drag a pair of horfes after it, when one horfe

is

is fufficient to take a cow or a bull. When he is purfued, he opens his way through the thickeft woods and coppices, breaking down every thing that oppof~s him. I do not know whether there have ever been any attempts to tame this animal, though it is by no means fierce, and does no mif-chief but to the chacras, or plantations, and might be of great fervice, on account of it's ftrength, if it could be brought to labour.

There are no wild horfes in this country, but the tame ones bred here are fuperior, both in beauty and ftrength, to any in South America; enduring long journeys, without any other provifion than what they pick up by the way; and in courage and fwiftnefs they are exceeded by none. There is alfo plenty of fmall game, and the Indians, who are very numerous, live chiefly upon it. There are likewife confi-derable quantities of the occidental bezoar, found not only in the ftomach of the guanacoes and vicunias, but alfo of the anta; though in this laft it is fomewhat coarfer. When it is given in a confiderable quantity, it greatly promotes a dia-phorefis. I have almoft always found it give relief and im-mediate eafe in heartburns, faintings, &c. the dofe confifting of a dram, or two fcruples, taken in any thing; though it might be given in a larger quantity with great fafety. I have found it preferable, in many cafes, to our teftaceous pow-ders, and mineral fubftances. I have had fome of thefe ftones that weighed eighteen ounces each.

There are many fpecies of the fowl kind, fuch as doves, turtles, ducks, pheafants, partridges, &c. which I mention, as profitable, though not regarded or ufed by the Indians. There are alfo birds of prey, as eagles, vultures, kites, gleads, owls, and falcons. But, fo far to the fouth, there are neither lions nor tigers, except in the Cordillera.

The

The country of the Huilliches, over againſt the Tehuel Mapu, and to the ſouth of Valdivia, is, according to the relations of the miſſionaries, a very poor country, and deſtitute of all the common neceſſaries of life; as indeed is all that ſea-coaſt below Chili, to the Magellanic Straits. The people of the coaſt live chiefly upon fiſh, and are diſtinguiſhed by the names of Chonos, Poy-yus, and Key-yus. Of theſe two laſt nations, thoſe who live farther from the coaſt hunt on foot, being very nimble, and inured to this exerciſe from their infancy. In Chiloe, great part of the proviſions for the miſſionaries, and the garriſon of Spaniſh ſoldiers, is ſent from Valdivia, or other ſeaports of Chili.

In this iſland there is a ſmall city, or rather village, called Caſtro ; where a Spaniſh captain, or deputy governor, reſides.

The mountains of the Huilliches are conſiderably lower than thoſe towards the north, ſo that they are in this country paſſable at all times of the year, and beſides have frequent openings. They are well covered with wood and even timber. There is a kind of tree peculiar to this country, which the Indians call lahual, and the Spaniards, alerce, or, according to our pronunciation, lawal and alerſey. It was not very particularly deſcribed to me ; but I take it to be of the fir kind. What is very remarkable in it, is it's convenience for being ſplit into boards, it's trunk being naturally marked with ſtraight lines from top to bottom ; ſo that, by cleaving it with wedges, it may be parted into very ſtraight boards, of any thickneſs, in a better and ſmoother manner than if they were ſawn. Theſe trees are very large, as I have been informed ; but I cannot pretend to ſay what is their general diameter.

If plants or ſeeds of this tree were brought over into
England,

England, it is very probable they would thrive here, the climate being as cold as in the countries where it grows; and it is there reckoned to be the moſt valuable timber they have, both for it's beauty and duration. It may not be improper to obſerve in this place, that by means of the rivers of Nahuelhuaupi, Sanquel, and Lolgen, great quantities of this wood, pine-trees, &c. might be ſent down, in large floats, to the Great River of Sauces, and ſo to the Bay of San Matthias, for the building of ſhips, houſes, &c.

The Huilliches have alſo a ſpecies of tobacco, which they bruiſe when almoſt green, and make into ſhort, thick, cylindrical rolls. It is of a dark-green colour, and when ſmoked yields a ſtrong, diſagreeable ſmell, ſomething different from the Virginia tobacco. It is very ſtrong, and ſoon intoxicates; ſo that they hand the pipe from one to another, and each takes a whiff in his turn, as the continuing it for any length of time would diſturb the ſenſes.

The country of thoſe Tehuelhets that live nearer and cloſe up to the Straits, as the Sehuau-cunnees, and Yacana-cunnees, is much the ſame as of the other Tehuelhets. They have within land ſome high woods, and a ſmall ſhrub, which produces a fruit very like our winberries, but ſomething hotter: they are good to eat, and very proper for the climate.

The Tierra del Fuego is compoſed of a great number of iſlands. Thoſe to the weſt are ſmall and low, full of marſhes and fens, and moſtly uninhabitable, being often covered with water; but thoſe which are to the eaſt are bigger, and higher land, with mountains and woods, and are inhabited by Indians of the Yacana-cunnees, and theſe have had frequent communication with the French and Spaniards, who went thither from the Malouin Iſlands to get wood. I cannot

not pretend to say, whether in these large islands there is any game, besides that of fowl: but it is highly credible, that the Indians who dwell there do not live entirely upon fish, which it is very difficult to take during the winter in these cold climates.

In the year 1765 or 1766 (I do not remember which) a Spanish ship, laden with merchandize for Peru, was driven ashore and beat to pieces upon the Island del Fuego, about fourteen leagues (as they reckoned) from the Straits mouth. The crew being saved, they made themselves a vessel, big enough to carry them and their provisions to Buenos-Ayres; where they informed the Governor, Don Pedro de Cevallos, that the Indians, natives of this island, were very humane and hospitable, and helped them to carry down many very heavy trees, which they had fallen for the building of their vessel, and assisted them in every thing: that they had been very liberal of their cargo to the Indians, who esteemed those things least which were of the greatest value, as silk, satin, tissues, &c. and were more desirous of the coarsest cloths, to keep them warm: that at first they came down in great numbers with their arms, bows and arrows, and that their manner of expressing a desire of friendship and peace was by laying down their arms, bowing their bodies, and then leaping up and rubbing their bellies, or beating on them with their hands. The Governor sent this account to the Court of Spain, and proposed the fixing a colony in this island; but the French being at that time tampering with the Spanish Court about the purchase of the Malouin Islands, the prudent designs of the Governor were frustrated, and he was recalled to his own country.

Tamu, the Yacana-cunnee Cacique, told me that they used a kind of float, with which they sometimes passed the Straits, and

and had communication with thofe of his nation: from whence it is evident, that this place has the conveniences of wood, water, and foil; and, if there could be found a tolerable harbour, it would be much more convenient for a colony, and have a better command of the paffage to the South Sea, than Falkland's Iflands.

The Malouin or Falkland's Iflands are many in number; fome are exceeding fmall; but there are two which are very large. What I fhall relate concerning them is according to the accounts which I have received from many of the Spanifh officers, who went to receive this country from the French, and to tranfport the Spaniards thither from Buenos-Ayres, as well as to carry away the French inhabitants; and alfo from a French gunner, who failed with me from the River of Plata to the Port of Cadiz, and had refided in thofe iflands feveral years. All thefe were unexceptionable witneffes.

Thefe iflands are fo low and boggy, that after a fhower of rain it is impoffible to ftir out, without finking up to the knees in mire. The houfes are built with earth, and from the exceeding moiftnefs of the country, are green within with mofs; and bricks cannot be made for want of fuel. The fettlers have fown various kinds of grain, as corn, barley, peafe, beans, &c. but the land is fo barren, that they all run into grafs and ftraw, and yield no crop. All the induftry of the French, for feveral years, could only accomplifh the raifing a fmall quantity of falad; and this they effected by gathering the dung of all their animals; cows, hogs, and horfes. The only animals which are natural to thefe iflands are penguins and buftards, and thefe laft are alone eatable. They are but indifferent food, are killed by fhooting, and foon grew fo fhy, that they became very dear. Some fifh are alfo taken, but in quantities by no means pro-

B b portionable

portionable to the wants of the inhabitants. So great is the poverty of the country, that the Spanish Governor of Buenos-Ayres was obliged to be at the expense of sending ships every three or four months, to maintain the people and garrison, without any returns; and though live hogs, cows, and horses, have been carried thither, yet the country is so cold, so moist, and so barren of shelter, that they never increase; so that these charges must last as long as the settlement continues. There is no wood, and nothing that serves for fuel but a low shrub, something like our furze or heath, and this but in small quantities: the inhabitants therefore are obliged to send small vessels to fetch wood from Tierra del Fuego. Water is almost the only necessary this country affords, besides the convenience of a good harbour; which yet does not appear to answer the end for which the settlement was made: for as this Haven of Solidad lies open to the north or north east, a ship must have a wind from that quarter, to enter it. Now as such a wind is the most favourable for passing Cape Horn, a ship would hardly enter here, and lose the favourable gale that would carry her into the South Sea; especially as she must wait for a contrary wind to get out again, and then for a north easterly wind to steer for Cape Horn; and all this in a place where there are no hopes of taking in any other provision besides water.

The French sent people to these islands in the time of the last war, to secure a port for their ships coming from the East Indies by the South Sea; which course they took at that time, to escape the English privateers: but when the war was over, being tired of so wretched a colony, and so many expenses, which now ceased to answer, they determined to leave them. But being desirous (if possible) to recover the money laid out here, they represented their new acquisitions

in

in fo favourable a manner to the Spanifh Court, that the King of Spain agreed to pay five hundred thoufand dollars (fome fay eight hundred thoufand, and others enlarge the fum to a million) for their ceding them to Spain: whereof the King of France was to receive a part, and the reft to go to Monfieur Bougainville the proprietor; befides fome cargoes of goods, bought with this money in the Rio Janeiro, permitted to be fold in Buenos-Ayres. All this the captain of a Spanifh frigate reprefented, with a great deal of freedom, to the prefent Governor of Buenos-Ayres, in the prefence of Monfieur Bougainville; complaining of the trick put upon the King of Spain, and protefting that no perfon, commiffioned to receive thefe iflands, could, confiftently with the loyalty he owed his Sovereign, or his obligations as a Chriftian, upon feeing them, accept the delivery, till he had firft given an account of them to the Court of Spain; it being evident that they had been grofsly impofed upon. Monfieur Bougainville did not think proper to contradict what this officer had faid; who, befides being an unexceptionable eye-witnefs himfelf, could (if neceffary) have corroborated his account by the teftimonies of a hundred people, who were lately arrived with the exportation of the French inhabitants.

The Spaniards tranfported with their colony two Francifcan friars, and a governor or vice-governor; who, beholding their fettlement, were overwhelmed with grief; and the Governor, Colonel Catani, at the departure of the fhips for Buenos-Ayres, with tears in his eyes declared, that he thought thofe happy who got from fo miferable a country, and that he himfelf fhould be very glad if he was permitted to throw up his commiffion, and return to Buenos-Ayres, though in no higher ftation than that of a cabin-boy.

CHAPTER

CHAPTER IV.

An Account of the Inhabitants of the most Southern Part of
AMERICA, *described in the Map.*

THE nations of Indians, which inhabit these parts, bear among themselves the general denominations of Moluches and Puelches.

The Moluches are known among the Spaniards by the names of Aucaes and Araucanos.

The former of these is a nick-name, and a word of reproach, meaning rebel, wild, savage, or banditti; the word aucani signifying to rebel, rise, or make a riot, and is applied both to men and beasts, as auca cahual is a wild horse, aucatun, or aucatuln, to make an uproar.

They call themselves Moluches, from the word molun, to wage war; and moluche signifies a warriour. They are dispersed over the country both on the east and west sides of the Cordillera of Chili, from the confines of Peru to the Straits of Magellan, and may be divided into the different nations of the Picunches, Pehuenches, and Huilliches.

The Picunches are the most northern of these people, and are so called from picun, which in their language signifies north, and che, men or people. They inhabit the mountains, from Coquimbo to somewhat lower than St. Jago of Chili. These are the most valiant and the biggest-bodied men of all the Moluches; especially those to the west of the
Cordillera:

Cordillera: among which are thofe of Penco, Tucapel; and Arauco; from which laft, the Spaniards by miftake gave the name of Araucanos to all the reft of the Indians of Chili. Thofe who live to the eaft of the Cordillera reach fomething lower than Mendoza, and are called by thofe on the other fide Puelches, puel fignifying eaft. But by others who live towards the fouth, they are called Picunches. I knew fome of their Caciques; whofe names were Tfeucan-antu, Pilque-pangi, Caru-pangi, and Caru-lonco.

The Pehuenches border on the Picunches to the north, and reach from over againft Valdivia to thirty five degrees of fouth latitude. They derive their name from the word pehuen, which fignifies pine-tree; becaufe their country abounds with thefe trees. As they live to the fouth of the Picunches, they are fometimes called by them Huilliches, or Southern People, but moft generally Pehuenches. Their Caciques were Colopichun, Amolepi, Nonque, Nicolafquen, Guenulep, Cufu-huanque, Col-nancon, Ayalep and Antu-cule. The laft was a young Cacique, whom I knew very well.

Thefe two nations were formerly very numerous, and were engaged in long and bloody wars with the Spaniards, whom they almoft drove out of Chili, deftroyed the cities of the Imperial, Oforno, and Villarica, and killed two of their prefidents, Valdivia, and Don Martin de Loyola; but they are now fo much diminifhed, as not to be able to mufter four thoufand men among them all. This has been in fome mea-fure owing to their frequent wars with the Spaniards of Chili, Mendoza, Cordova, and Buenos-Ayres, with their neigh-bours the Puelches, and with one another. But what has made the greateft havock amongft them, is the brandy which they buy of the Spaniards, and their pulcu, or chicha, which they make themfelves. They often pawn and fell

their

their wives and children to the Spaniards for brandy, with
which they get drunk, and then kill one another; and it
seldom happens that the party who has suffered most on
these occasions waits long for an opportunity of revenge.
The small pox also, which was introduced into this country
by the Europeans, causes a more terrible destruction among
them than the plague, desolating whole towns by it's malig-
nant effects. This disorder is much more fatal to these people,
than to the Spaniards or Negroes, owing to their gross habit
of body, bad food, and want of covering, medicines, and
necessary care: for the nearest relations of those who fall
sick fly from them, to avoid the distemper, and leave them
to perish, perhaps in the middle of a desart. About forty
five years ago, the numerous nation of the Chechehets, having caught this disorder in the neighbourhood of Buenos-
Ayres, endeavoured to fly from it, by retiring into their own
country, which was about two hundred leagues distant,
through vast desarts. During this journey they daily left behind them their sick friends and relations, forsaken and alone,
with no other assistance than a hide reared up against the
wind, and a pitcher of water. Thus they have been brought
so low, that they have not more than three hundred men capable of bearing arms.

The Huilliches, or Southern Moluches, reach from Valdivia to the Straits of Magellan. They are divided into four
distinct tribes or nations. The first of these reaches to the
Sea of Chiloe, and beyond the Lake of Nahuelhuaupi, and
speak the Chilenian tongue. The second nation are the
Chonos, who live on and near the islands of Chiloe. The
third nation is called Poy-yus, or Peyes, and inhabits the seacoast from forty eight to a little more than fifty one degrees of
south latitude: and from thence to the Straits live the fourth
nation,

nation, called the Key-yus, or Keyes. Thefe laft three nations are known by the name of Vuta Huilliches, or Great Huilliches, becaufe they are bigger-bodied men than the firft, who are called Pichi Huilliches, or Little Huilliches. They feem likewife to be a different people; as the language they fpeak is a mixture of the Moluche and Tehuel languages. The other Huilliches, and the Pehuenches, fpeak in the fame manner with one another, and differ only from the Picunches in ufing the letter S inftead of R and D, not having thefe two letters in their alphabet: and the Picunches, having no S, ufe R and D inftead of it; and oftentimes T, where the others ufe CH; as domo, for fomo, a woman; huaranca. for huafanca, a thoufand; vuta, for vucha, great. Thefe nations are numerous, efpecially the Vuta Huilliches. The Caciques of the firft, or Pichi Huilliches, were Puelman, Painiacal, Tepuanca; whom I have feen; with many others, whofe names I have forgotten.

The Puelches, or Eaftern People (fo called by thofe of Chili becaufe they live to the eaft of them) are bounded on the weft by the Moluches, down to the Straits of Magellan; by which they are terminated on the fouth; on the north, by the Spaniards of Mendoza, San Juan, San Louis de la Punta, Cordova, and Buenos-Ayres; and to the eaft, by the ocean. They bear different denominations, according to the fituation of their refpective countries, or becaufe they were originally of different nations. Thofe towards the north are called Taluhets; to the weft and fouth of thefe are the Diuihets; to the fouth eaft, the Chechehets; and to the fouth of thefe laft is the country of the Tehuelhets, or, in their proper language, Tehuel-Kunny, i. e. Southern Men.

The Taluhets border to the weft on the Picunches, and dwell on the eaft fide of the Firft Defaguadero, as far as

the

the lakes of Guanacache, in the jurifdictions of St. Juan and St. Louis de la Punta, fcattered in fmall troops, and feldom fixed to one place. There are alfo fome few of them in the jurifdiction of Cordova, on the Rivers Quarto, Tercero, and Segundo; but the greater part are either deftroyed by their wars with the other Puelches and the Mocovies, or have taken refuge with the Spaniards. There were formerly fome of this nation in the diftrict of Buenos-Ayres, on the rivers of Lujan and Conchas, and that of the Matanza; but they are now no more. Their Caciques were Mugeloop, Alcochoro, Galelian, and Mayu.

Of this nation fo few remain at prefent, that they are fcarce able to raife two hundred fighting men, and only make a kind of piratical war in fmall parties, except when they are affifted by their neighbours, the Picunches, Pehuenches, and Diuihets; and, even with all their auxiliaries, cannot bring into the field above five hundred men at the moft, and feldom fo many. This nation, and that of the Diuihets, are known to the Spaniards by the name of Pampas.

The Diuihets border weftwardly upon the country of the Pehuenches, from thirty five to thirty eight degrees of fouthern latitude, and extend, along the rivers Sanquel, Colorado, and Hueyque, to within about forty miles of the Cafuhati on the eaft. They are of the fame wandering difpofition with the Taluhets, and are not much more numerous, having been greatly deftroyed in their attempts to plunder the Spaniards; fometimes taking part with the Taluhets, at other times with the Pehuenches, and frequently making their excurfions alone, on the frontiers of the mountains of Cordova and Buenos-Ayres, from the Arrecife to Lujan; killing the men, taking the women and children for flaves,

and

and driving away the cattle. The Caciques of this nation, were Concalcac, Pichivele, Yahati, and Doenoyal.

These two nations subsist chiefly on the flesh of mares, which they hunt, in small companies of about thirty or forty each, in the vast plains betwixt Mendoza and Buenos-Ayres; where they often meet with large troops of Spaniards, sent out on purpose, who execute the laws of retaliation with at least equal cruelty. But this is not the only danger which they run the risk of: for if the Tehuelhets, or Chechehets, have reached the Casuhati, or the Vuulcan and Tandil, at the time when the Diuihets and Taluhets are about to retire with their booty, they continue to fall on them in their retreat (particularly in places where the length of the march obliges them to halt for some time to rest their cattle) kill all that resist, strip the rest of every thing, and carry away the plunder.

The country of the Chechehets, or People of the East, lies properly between the River Hueyque and the First Desaguadero, or River Colorado, and from thence to the Second Desaguadero, or Black River; but they are perpetually wandering about, and move their habitations, and separate, for the most trifling motives, and oftentimes from no other reason, but their natural propensity to roving. Their country abounds only in the lesser kinds of game, as hares, armadilloes, ostriches, &c. producing few or no guanacoes. When they go up to the mountains of the Tandil and the Casuhati, on account of the scarcity of horses, they are so very unskilful in hunting, &c. that they never bring back any on their return, unless their neighbours the Tehuelhets give them some, or they have the good fortune to surprise some of the parties of the Pehuenches, who generally return well provided. In other respects, they are a poor, harmless, and sincere people, and more honest than the

Moluches

Moluches or the Taluhets. They are very fuperftitious, extremely addicted to divinations and witchcraft, and are eafily deceived. They are in general a tall, ftout race of people, like their neighbours the Tehuelhets; but they fpeak a different language. Although they are mild and humble in peace, they are bold and active in war, as the Taluhets and Diuihets have often found to their coft; but now they are reduced to a very fmall number, having been deftroyed by the fmall pox. Their furviving Caciques were Sejechu and Daychaco.

The Tehuelhets, who in Europe are known by the name of Patagons, have been, through ignorance of their idiom, called Tehuelchus: for chu fignifies country or abode, and not people; which is expreffed by the word het, and, more to the fouth, by the word kunnee or kunny. Thefe and the Chechehets are known to the Spaniards by the name of Serranos, or Mountaineers. They are fplit into a great many fubdivifions, as the Leuvuches, or People of the River, and Calille-Het, or People of the Mountains; amongft whom are the Chulilau-cunnees, Sehuau-cunnees, and Yacana-cunnees. All thefe, except thofe of the River, are called by the Moluches, Vucha-Huilliches.

The Leuvuches live on the north and fouth banks of the River Negro, or, as they call it, Cufu Leuvu. To the north they have a large, uninhabited country, which is quite impaffable from thick woods and lakes, and marfhes, which are full of thorny, ftrong canes, which they call fanquel. Thus all communication is fhut up from the north, but by marching weftward, by the foot of the Cordillera, or eaftward, by the feacoaft. This people feem to be compofed of the Tehuelhets and Chechehets, but fpeak the language of the latter, with a fmall mixture of the Tehuel tongue.

tongue. On the eaftern fide, they reach to the Chechehets; on the weftern, they join to the Pehuenches and Huilliches; to the north, they border on the Diuihets; and, to the fouth, on the other Tehuelhets. Going round the great Lake Huechun Lavquen, they reach Valdivia in fix days journey from Huichin. This nation feem to be the head of the Chechehets and Tehuelhets, and their Caciques, Cacapol and his fon Cangapol, are a kind of petty monarchs over all the reft. When they declare war, they are immediately joined by the Chechehets, Tehuelhets, and Huilliches, and by thofe Pehuenches who live moft to the fouth, a little lower than Valdivia.

Of themfelves they are but few in number, it being with the greateft difficulty that they are able to raife three hundred fighting men, having been greatly leffened by the fmall pox which reduced the Chechehets: for, having joined that nation, they came to the plains of Buenos-Ayres in great numbers, and attacked the famous Don Gregorio Mayu Pilqui Ya, upon the Lake of the Lobos, with a ftrong party of Taluhets; all of whom they cut off, and then retreated to the Vuulcan: but unfortunately they carried away with them fome cloaths, which a fhort time before had been bought at Buenos-Ayres, and were tainted with the fmall pox. They have likewife been very much diminifhed in their wars with their northern neighbours, the Picunches, Pehuenches, and Taluhets; who, combining together, fometimes come down upon them by the fide of the Cordillera and furprife them. Whenever this happens, they avoid their enemies by fwimming acrofs the river, which the others are not able to do. But the children, which in the hurry and confufion of flight are left behind, fall a prey to the inhuman enemy; who cruelly butcher all they find, not

fparing

fparing even thofe who hang up in their cradles. Thefe attacks however are not always fo fecret, but that they fome-times have advice of them, and then few efcape the fury of this brave nation; and their Cacique Cacapol fhews to his guefts great heaps of bones, fkulls, &c. of thefe enemies, whom he boafts to have flain. The policy of this Cacique is to maintain peace with the Spaniards, that his people may hunt with fecurity in the vaft plains of Buenos-Ayres, between the frontiers of the Matanza, Conchas, and Mag-dalena, and the mountains: for which reafon he does not fuffer the other tribes to come down lower than Lujan, to maintain peace on the fouthern fide. Wherefore his Caciques and confederates, in the months of July, Auguft, and September, place themfelves to hunt, where they may watch the motions of their enemies; whom they often attack and deftroy. On this account thefe Indians never made war upon the Spaniards (though extremely jealous of them) till about 1738 or 1740; when the caufes of the difpute were as follows.

The Spaniards, very injudicioufly, and indeed ungrate-fully, drove Mayu Pilqui-Ya, the only Taluhet Cacique who was their friend, to his deftruction, by forcing him to retire to a diftance, expofed to the enemies which he had gained by defending their territories from the reft of his countrymen and the Picunches, and too far off to receive any fuccours from themfelves. After the death of this Cacique, a party of Taluhets and Picunches attacked the farms of the Rivers Areco and Arecife, led on by Tfeucanantu and Carulonco; and the Spaniards, with their Maeftre de Campo, Don Juan de St. Martin, being too late to overtake the robbers, turned to the fouthward, that they might not return empty-handed. Here they met with the tents of the old Caleliyan, with one

half

half of his people, who, entirely ignorant of what had happened, were sleeping without suspicion of danger. Without examining if these were the aggressors, they fired upon them while they lay asleep in their tents, and killed many of them, with their wives and children. The rest, being awakened, and beholding the sad spectacle of their slaughtered wives and children, were resolved not to survive the loss of them, and snatching up their arms, sold their lives as dearly as they could; but, in the end, they and their Cacique were all put to the sword.

The young Caleliyan was at that time absent, but having notice of what had happened, returned upon the retreat of the Spaniards, and beholding the slaughter of his father, relations, and friends, resolved on immediate vengeance; and raising about three hundred men, among his countrymen and the Picunches, fell upon the village of Lujan, killed a great number of Spaniards, took some captives, and drove away some thousands of cattle. Upon this, the Spaniards raised about six hundred of their militia, and a troop of regulars, with all expedition, but not soon enough for so swift an enemy. Not being able to overtake him, they turned round by the salt ponds, and fell down to the Casuhati, where the Cacique Cangapol was at that time, with a few Indians, who prudently retired. Being disappointed here, they returned by the sea side, towards the Vuulcan, where they met a troop of Huilliches; who, being friends and at peace, went without arms to receive them, not having the least suspicion of any danger; but by the order of the Maestre del Campo they were quickly surrounded and cut in pieces, although the military officer of the troop remonstrated against such a proceeding, and interceded in their behalf. Having performed this exploit, they marched to the Salado, not above

forty

forty leagues from the city, and about twenty from the farms of Buenos-Ayres; where a Tehuel Cacique, called Tolmichi-ya, coufin to Cacapol, and the friend and ally of the Spaniards, and much refpected by them, was encamped, under the protection of the then Governor Salcedo. This Cacique, with the Governor's letter in his hand, and fhewing his licenfe, was fhot through the head by the Maeftre del Campo; all the Indian men were killed, and the women and children made captives, with the youngeft fon of the Cacique, a boy of about twelve years of age. His eldeft fon very fortunately was gone out two days before, to hunt wild horfes, with a party of Indians.

This cruel conduct of the Maeftre del Campo fo exafpe-rated all the Indian nations of Puelches and Moluches, that they all took arms againft the Spaniards; who found them-felves attacked at once, from the frontiers of Cordova and Santa Fe, down the whole length of the River of Plate, on a frontier of a hundred leagues; and in fuch a manner, that it was impoffible to defend themfelves: for the Indians, in fmall flying parties, falling on many villages or farms at the fame time, and generally by moon-light, it was impoffible to tell the numbers of their parties; fo that while the Spa-niards purfued them in great numbers on one part, they left all the reft unguarded.

Cacapol, who, with his Tehuelhets, as yet had lived in friendfhip with the Spaniards, was highly irritated at the at-tempt made on his fon, the flaughter of his friends the Huilliches, the murder of his beft-beloved kinfman and other relations, and the unworthy manner in which their dead bodies had been treated; and though he was at that time near feventy years of age, he took the field at the head of a thoufand men (fome fay four thoufand) confifting of

Tehuelhets,

Tehuelhets, Huilliches, and Pehuenches, and fell upon the District of the Magdalen, about four leagues distant from Buenos-Ayres, and divided his troops with so much judgment, that he scoured and dispeopled, in one day and a night, above twelve leagues of the most populous and plentiful country in these parts. They killed many Spaniards, and took a great number of women and children captives, with above twenty thousand head of cattle, besides horses, &c. In this expedition the Indians lost only one Tehuelhet, who, straggling from the rest in hopes of plunder, fell into the hands of the Spaniards. Cangapol, the son of Cacapol, was pursued and overtaken; but the Spaniards had not the courage to attack him, though at that time double in number, both they and their horses being quite tired with their expeditious march of forty leagues, without taking any refreshment.

The inhabitants of Buenos-Ayres, having early notice from the fugitives of this unexpected attack, were in the most terrible consternation; many of the military officers ran about the streets bare-headed, in a state of distraction, and the churches and religious houses were filled with people, who had taken shelter in them, as if the enemy had been in the city. The Spaniards, humbled by this blow, deprived the Field-Marshal of his commission, and appointed another, and then raised an army of seven hundred men; which marched to the Casuhati, not to renew the war, but to sue for peace. A whole year had now elapsed since their last defeat, and the Indians, with their young Cacique Cangapol at their head, had raised another army, from all the different nations, consisting of near four thousand men; with which they might have cut all the Spaniards in pieces: yet, notwithstanding these advantages, they listened to the proposal of
the

the new Field-Marfhal, whom they confidered as their
friend; who, fearful of the confequences which might attend a frefh rupture, offered, among other conditions, to
deliver up all the Indian captives without any confideration
whatfoever, and that the Spanifh captives fhould be ranfomed.
The indignity of this condition was ftrongly reprefented by
the Jefuit Miffionary, who, with fome of his Chechehet and
Tehuel Converts, went with the Spanifh camp, and by whofe
means chiefly the Indians were prevailed upon to fpare the
Spanifh army. He propofed that there fhould be a mutual
exchange of prifoners; but fo great was the fear of another
war, that his advice was rejected, though many of the Indians
did not defire more honourable conditions. Some Tehuel
Caciques, who had brought their captives along with them,
immediately delivered them up, on making peace, not underftanding the propofal of the Field-Marfhal in any other
light, than that the delivery of prifoners was to be reciprocal.
The Moluches indeed went to Buenos-Ayres, and recovered
all the Indian prifoners, as well as thofe of the Tehuelhets,
without returning the captives they had taken from the
Spaniards. Since this time, the Tehuelhets, allured by the
hopes of plunder, have once a year made incurfions into the
territory of Buenos-Ayres, and carried away great numbers
of cattle. However this was the utmoft damage they ever
did, till the year 1767; when, having received fome provo-
cation, they renewed the war, and carried away many captives; and of two parties of Spaniards who purfued them ten
only efcaped. A greater body of troops, with all the militia
of Buenos-Ayres, and fome companies of regulars, with
their Colonel Catani, afterwards overtook them, but thought
it prudent to let them go unmolefted, for fear of fharing the
fate of their companions.

The

The Tehuelhets that border all along, from eaſt to weſt, on thoſe of the River of Sauces, are bounded on the north eaſt by the Chechehets, and on the eaſt by a vaſt deſart, which begins at about forty leagues from the mouth of the Black River towards the ſouth, and extends almoſt to the Straits of Magellan. To the weſtward, they border on the Huilliches who inhabit the ſeacoaſts of Chiloe, and extend to forty four degrees of ſouthern latitude. All their country is mountainous, with deep vallies, and has no conſiderable rivers. The natives are ſupplied with water from ſprings and ſmall rivulets, which end in lakes, where they water their cattle. In dry ſummers theſe lakes are empty, and then they are obliged to go for water to the Black River or elſe-where. This nation neither ſow nor plant, but live chiefly on guanacoes, hares, and oſtriches, which their country affords, and on mares fleſh, when they can get it.

The ſcarcity of this food occaſions them to be in perpetual motion, from one country to another, to ſeek for it: ſo that they go, in great numbers, ſometimes to the Caſuhati; at other times, to the mountains of Vuulcan or Tandil, and the plains near Buenos-Ayres; which is three or four hundred leagues from their own country. Of all nations upon earth, there is no account of any ſo reſtleſs, and who have ſuch a diſpoſition to roving as theſe people: for neither extreme old-age, blindneſs, nor any other diſtemper, pre-vents them from indulging this inclination to wander. They are a very ſtrong, well-made people, and not ſo tawny as the other Indians: ſome of their women are even as white as the Spaniards. They are courteous, obliging, and good-natured; but very inconſtant, and not to be relied on in their pro-miſes and engagements. They are ſtout, warlike, and fear-leſs of death. They are by much the moſt numerous of all

F f

the

the Indian nations of thefe parts, and are as many as all the reft put together. They are the enemies of the Moluches, and extremely feared by them; and if they had been as well provided with horfes as the Moluches, the latter, who are fo terrible to the Spaniards, would have been long fince deftroyed; nor would the Diuihets and Taluhets have been able to have withftood their power.

To the fouth of thefe live the Chulilau-cunnees and Sehuau-cunnees, which are the moft fouthern Indians who ride on horfeback. Sehuau fignifies, in the Tehuel dialect, a fpecies of black rabbit, about the fize of a field-rat; and as their country abounds in thefe animals, their name may be derived from thence; cunnee fignifying people.

The two laft-mentioned nations appear to be the fame people with the other Tehuelhets, and differ little in their idiom. The fmall difference there is may be owing to the communication they have with the Poy-yus and Key-yus, who live upon the weftern coaft and the ftraits.

All the Tehuelhets fpeak a different language from the other Puelches and the Moluches, and this difference does not only include words, but alfo the declinations and conjugations of them; though they ufe fome of the words of both nations. For example, for a mountain they fay calille; the Moluches, calel; but the Puelches, cafu. Pichua is the Tehuel name for a guanaco, but has no likenefs to Iuhuan, or huanque, in the Molu tongue: nor yagip, water, to co: nor yagiu, watering-place, to cohue; nor cunnee, people, to che or het. I am inclined to think that thefe nations of Tehuelhets are thofe which the Miffionaries of Chili have called Poy-yus, as they live in the fituation in
which

which they place the Poy-yus: but the truth is that the Poy-yus
live nearer the feacoaft.

The laft of the Tehuel nations are the Yacana-cunnees,
which fignifies foot-people; for they always travel on foot,
having no horfes in their country. To the north, they
border on the Sehuau-cunnees; to the weft, on the Key-yus,
or Key-yuhues, from whom they are divided by a ridge of
mountains: to the eaft, they are bounded by the ocean; and
to the fouth, by the iflands of Tierra del Fuego, or the
South Sea. Thefe Indians live near the fea, on both fides of
the ftraits, and oftentimes make war with one another. They
make ufe of light floats, like thofe of Chiloe, in order to
pafs the ftraits. They are fometimes attacked by the Huilliches, and the other Tehuelhets, who carry them away for
flaves, as they have nothing to lofe but their liberty and
their lives. They live chiefly on fifh; which they catch,
either by diving, or ftriking them with their darts. They
are very nimble of foot, and catch guanacoes and oftriches
with their bowls. Their ftature is much the fame as that
of the other Tehuelhets, rarely exceeding feven feet,
and oftentimes not fix feet. They are an innocent, harmlefs
people.

When the French or Spaniards go (as they frequently do)
to the Tierra del Fuego, to get fuel for the Malouin fettlements, thefe people give them all the affiftance in their
power. To invite them down, they always make ufe of a
white flag, that they may be known; for fuch impreffions
have they received of the Englifh, that on feeing a red
flag they always run away. The French and Spaniards attribute this to fome Englifh veffels having fired fome great
guns; the report of which, they fuppofe, frightened the
Indians to fuch a degree, that they never dared to appear

fince

fince, on feeing the red colours. This may have been the cafe; but it is certain many artifices have been made ufe of, to prevent their having any communication with the Englifh. A Cacique of this nation, who came with the other Tehuel-hets to pay me a vifit, told me that he had been in a houfe of wood, that travelled on the water. As this was told me a few years after Admiral Anfon paffed to the South Sea, I concluded it might be one of the fhips belonging to his fquadron.

All thefe nations of the Tehuelhets are called, by the Moluches, Vucha-Huilliches, or Great Southern People: the Spaniards call them Mountaineers, though they are ig-norant from whence they come. To the reft of Europe they are known by the name of Patagonians.

As I mentioned in the introduction, I have feen Caciques of all the different nations of Indians inhabiting the fouthern part of America, and obferved that the Puelches, or Eaftern Indians, were a large race of people, and feveral of them near feven feet fix inches high: but thefe are not a diftinct race; for I have feen others, of the fame family, who were not above fix feet high. The Moluches, or Weftern Indians, who live among the mountains, are rather of low ftature, but broad and thick-fet. The inhabitants of the foggy moun-tains of the Cordillera are often guilty of fuicide; a crime feldom heard of among the Eaftern Indians.

The names of their Caciques which I knew, were Caca-pol, Cangapol, Yampalco, Tolmichiya, Guelmen, Saufi-miyan, Yepelche, Marique, Chuyuentuya, Guerquen, Clufgell, Millarfuel, and Tamu.

The report that there is a nation in thefe parts defcended from Europeans, or the remains of fhipwrecks, is, I verily be-lieve, entirely falfe and groundlefs, and occafioned by mif-
underftanding

underftanding the accounts of the Indians. For if they are afked in Chili concerning any inland fettlement of Spaniards, they give an account of towns and white people, meaning Buenos Ayres, &c. and fo vice verfa; not having the leaft idea, that the inhabitants of thefe two diftant countries are known to each other. Upon my queftioning the Indians on this fubject, I found my conjecture to be right; and they acknowledged, upon my naming Chiloe, Valdivia, &c. (at which they feemed amazed) that thofe were the places they had mentioned under the defcription of European fettlements.

What further makes this fettlement of the Cæfares to be altogether incredible, is the moral impoffibility that even two or three hundred Europeans, almoft all men, without having any communication with a civilized country, could penetrate through fo many warlike and numerous nations, and maintain themfelves as a feparate republic, in a country which produces nothing fpontaneoufly, and where the inhabitants live only by hunting; and all this for the fpace of two hundred years (as the ftory is told) without being extirpated, either by being killed, or made flaves by the Indians, or without lofing all European appearances by intermarrying with them. And befides, there is not a foot of all this continent, that the wandering nations do not ramble over every year; for even the uninhabited defart, which is wafhed by the Atlantic Ocean, is travelled over every year, to bury the dry bones of the dead, and to look for falt. Their Caciques, and others of the greateft repute for truth among them, have often protefted to me, that there are no white people in all thofe parts, except thofe which are known to all Europe; as in Chili, Buenos-Ayres, Chiloe, Mendoza, &c.

CHAPTER

CHAPTER V.

*The Religion, Government, Policy, and Cuſtoms, of the Moluches
and Puelches.*

THESE Indians believe in two ſuperior beings, the one good, the other evil. The good power is called by the Moluches Toquichen, which ſignifies governor of the people; by the Taluhets and Diuihets, Soychu, which, in their tongue, ſignifies the being who preſides in the land of ſtrong drink: the Tehuelhets call him Guayava-cunnee, or the lord of the dead.

They have formed a multiplicity of theſe deities; each of whom they believe to preſide over one particular caſt or family of Indians, of which he is ſuppoſed to have been the creator. Some make themſelves of the caſt of the tiger, ſome of the lion, ſome of the guanaco, and others of the oſtrich, &c. They imagine that theſe deities have each their ſeparate habitations, in vaſt caverns under the earth, beneath ſome lake, hill, &c. and that when an Indian dies, his ſoul goes to live with the deity who preſides over his particular family, there to enjoy the happineſs of being eternally drunk.

They believe that their good deities made the world, and that they firſt created the Indians in their caves, gave them the lance, the bow and arrows, and the ſtone-bowls, to fight and hunt with, and then turned them out to ſhift for themſelves.

felves. They imagine that the deities of the Spaniards did the fame by them, but that inftead of lances, bows, &c. they gave them guns and fwords. They fuppofe that when the beafts, birds, and leffer animals were created, thofe of the more nimble kind came immediately out of their caves, but that the bulls and cows being the laft, the Indians were fo frightened at the fight of their horns, that they ftopped up the entrance of their caves with great ftones. This is the reafon they give, why they had no black cattle in their country, till the Spaniards brought them over, who more wifely had let them out of the caves.

They have formed a belief that fome of them after death are to return to thefe divine caverns; and they fay alfo that the ftars are old Indians, that the milky way is the field where the old Indians hunt oftriches, and that the two fouthern clouds are the feathers of the oftriches which they kill. They have an opinion alfo that the creation is not yet exhaufted, nor all of it come out to the daylight of this upper world.

Their wizards, beating their drums, and rattling their cala-bafhes full of fea-fhells, pretend to fee, under ground, men, cattle, &c. with fhops of rum, brandy, cafcabels, and a va-riety of other things. But I am very well affured that they do not all of them believe this nonfenfe: for the Tehuel Cacique, Chehuentuya, came to me one morning, with an account of a new difcovery, made by one of their wizards, of one of thefe fubterraneous countries, which was under the place where we lived; and upon my laughing at, and expofing their fimplicity, in being impofed upon by fuch fables and foolifh ftories, he anfwered with fcorn, Epu-eungeing'n, They are old women's tales.

The Evil Principle is called by the Moluches Huecuvoe, or Huecuvu, that is, the Wanderer without. The Tehuelhets

elhets and Chechehets call him Atſkannakanatz, the other Puelches call him Valichu.

They acknowledge a great number of this kind of demons, wandering about the world, and attribute to them all the evil that is done in it, whether to man or beaſt; and they carry this opinion ſo far, as to believe that theſe unpropitious powers occaſion the wearineſs and fatigue which attends long journeys or hard labour. Each of their wizards is ſuppoſed to have two of theſe demons in conſtant attendance, who enable them to foretel future events; to diſcover what is paſſing, at the time preſent, at a great diſtance; and to cure the ſick, by fighting, driving away, or appeaſing, the other demons who torment them. They believe that the ſouls of their wizards, after death, are of the number of theſe demons.

Their worſhip is entirely directed to the evil being, except in ſome particular ceremonies made uſe of in reverence to the dead. To perform their worſhip, they aſſemble together in the tent of the wizard; who is ſhut up from the ſight of the reſt, in a corner of the tent. In this apartment, he has a ſmall drum, one or two round calabaſhes with ſmall ſea-ſhells in them, and ſome ſquare bags of painted hide, in which he keeps his ſpells. He begins the ceremony, by making a ſtrange noiſe with his drum and rattle-box; after which he feigns a fit, or ſtruggle with the devil, who it is then ſuppoſed has entered into him; keeps his eyes lifted up, diſtorts the features of his face, foams at the mouth, ſcrews up his joints, and, after many violent and diſtorting motions, remains ſtiff and motionleſs, reſembling a man ſeized with an epilepſy. After ſome time he comes to himſelf, as having got the better of the demon; next feigns, within his tabernacle, a faint, ſhrill, mournful voice, as of the evil ſpirit, who, by this diſmal cry, is ſuppoſed to
acknowledge

acknowledge himfelf fubdued; and then, from a kind of tripod, anfwers all queftions that are put to him. Whether his anfwers be true or falfe is of no great fignification; becaufe if his intelligence fhould prove falfe, it is the fault of the devil. On all thefe occafions the wizard is well paid.

The profeffion of the wizards is very dangerous, notwithftanding the refpect which is fometimes paid to them: for it often happens, when an Indian Chief dies, that fome of the wizards are killed; efpecially if they had any difpute with the deceafed juft before his death; the Indians, in this cafe, laying the lofs of their Chief upon the wizards and their demons. In cafes alfo of peftilence and epidemic diforders, when great numbers are carried off, the wizards often fuffer. On account of the fmallpox, which happened after the death of Mayu Pilqui-ya and his people, and almoft entirely deftroyed the Chechehets, Cangapol ordered all the wizards to be killed, to fee if by thefe means the diftemper would ceafe.

The wizards are of both fexes. The male wizards are obliged (as it were) to leave their fex, and to drefs themfelves in female apparel, and are not permitted to marry, though the female ones or witches may. They are generally chofen for this office when they are children, and a preference is always fhewn to thofe, who at that early time of life difcover an effeminate difpofition. They are cloathed very early in female attire, and prefented with the drum and rattles belonging to the profeffion they are to follow.

They who are feized with fits of the falling ficknefs, or the chorea Sancti Viti, are immediately felected for this employment, as chofen by the demons themfelves; whom they fuppofe to poffefs them, and to caufe all thofe convulfions and diftortions common in epileptic paroxyfms.

H h

The

The burial of their dead, and the superstitious reverence paid to their memory, are attended with great ceremony. When an Indian dies, one of the most distinguished women among them is immediately chosen, to make a skeleton of his body; which is done, by cutting out the entrails, which they burn to ashes, dissecting the flesh from the bones as clean as possible, and then burying them under ground, till the remaining flesh is entirely rotted off, or till they are removed (which must be within a year after the interment, but is sometimes within two months) to the proper burial-place of their ancestors.

This custom is strictly observed by the Moluches, Taluhets, and Diuihets; but the Chechehets and Tehuelhets, or Patagonians, place the bones on high, upon canes or twigs woven together, to dry and whiten with the sun and rain.

During the time that the ceremony of making the skeleton lasts, the Indians, covered with long mantles of skins, and their faces blackened with soot, walk round the tent, with long poles or lances in their hands; singing in a mournful tone of voice, and striking the ground, to frighten away the Valichus or Evil Beings. Some go to visit and console the widow, or widows, and other relations of the dead; that is, if there is any thing to be got; for nothing is done, but with a view of interest. During this visit of condolance, they cry, howl, and sing, in the most dismal manner; straining out tears, and pricking their arms and thighs with sharp thorns, to make them bleed. For this show of grief they are paid with glass beads, brass cascabels, and such like bawbles, which are in high estimation among them. The horses of the dead are also immediately killed, that he may have wherewithal to ride upon in the Alhue Mapu, or Country of the Dead; reserving only a few, to grace

the

the laft funeral pomp, and to carry the relicks to their proper fepulchres.

The widow, or widows, of the dead, are obliged to mourn
and faft for a whole year after the death of their hufband.
This confifts, in keeping themfelves clofe fhut up in their
tents, without having communication with any one, or ftirring
out, but for the common neceffaries of life; in not wafhing
their faces or hands, but being blackened with foot, and
having their garments of a mournful appearance; in ab-
ftaining from horfe's and cow's flefh, and, within-land, where
they are plenty, from the flefh of oftriches and guanacoes; but
they may eat any thing elfe. During the year of mourning
they are forbidden to marry, and if, within this time, a widow is difcovered to have had any communication with a
man, the relations of her dead hufband will kill them both;
unlefs it appears that fhe has been violated. But I did not
difcover that the men were obliged to any fuch kind of
mourning on the death of their wives.

When they remove the bones of their dead, they pack
them up together in a hide, and place them upon one of
the deceafed's favourite horfes, kept alive for that purpofe;
which they adorn after their beft fafhion, with mantles,
feathers, &c. and travel in this manner, though it be to the
diftance of three hundred leagues, till they arrive at the
proper burial-place, where they perform the laft ceremony.

The Moluches, Taluhets, and Diuihets, bury their dead
in large fquare pits, about a fathom deep. The bones are
put together, and fecured by tying each in their proper place,
then cloathed with the beft robes they can get, adorned with
beads, plumes, &c. all of which they cleanfe or change once a
year. They are placed in a row, fitting, with the fword, lance,
bow and arrows, bowls, and whatever elfe the deceafed had

while

while alive. Thefe pits are covered over with beams or trees, canes, or twigs woven together, upon which they put earth. An old matron is chofen out of each tribe, to take care of thefe graves, and on account of her employment is held in great veneration. Her office is, to open every year thefe dreary habitations, and to cloath and clean the fkeletons. Befides all this, they every year pour upon thefe graves fome bowls of their firft-made chica, and drink fome of it themfelves to the good health of the dead. Thefe burying places are, in general, not far diftant from their ordinary habitations; and they place all around the bodies of their dead horfes, raifed upon their feet, and fupported with fticks.

The Tehuelhets, or more fouthern Patagonians, differ in fome refpects from the other Indians. After having dried the bones of their dead, they carry them to a great diftance from their habitations, into the defert by the feacoaft, and after placing them in their proper form, and adorning them in the manner before defcribed, they fet them in order above ground, under a hut or tent, erected for that purpofe, with the fkeletons of their dead horfes placed around them.

In the expedition of the year 1746, fome Spanifh foldiers, with one of the miffionaries, travelling about thirty leagues within-land, to the weft of Port San Julian, found one of thefe Indian fepulchres, containing three fkeletons, and having as many dead horfes propped up round it.

It is not an eafy matter to trace any regular form of government, or civil conftitution, among thefe Indians: what little they have, feems to confift in a fmall degree of fubjection to their Caciques. The office of a Cacique is hereditary, not elective; and all the fons of a Cacique have a right to affume the dignity, if they can get any Indians to

follow

follow them; but, on account of the little use it is of to it's possessors, it is oftentimes resigned.

The Cacique has the power of protecting as many as apply to him, of composing or silencing any difference, or delivering over the offending party to be punished with death, without being accountable for it; for in these respects his will is the law. He is generally too apt to take bribes; delivering up his vassals, and even his relations, when well paid for it. According to his orders, the Indians encamp march, or travel from one place to another, to settle, hunt, or make war. He frequently summons them to his tent. and harangues them upon their behaviour, the exigencies of the time, the injuries they have received, the measures to be taken, &c. In these harangues, he always extols his own prowess and personal merit. When he is eloquent, he is greatly esteemed; and when a Cacique is not endowed with that accomplishment, he generally has an orator, who supplies his place. In cases of importance, especially those of war, he calls a council of the principal Indians and wizards; with whom he consults about the measures to be taken, to defend himself, or attack his enemies.

In a general war, when many nations enter into an alliance against a common enemy, they choose an Apo, or Commander in Chief, from among the oldest or most celebrated of the Caciques. But this honour, though elective, has for many years been in a manner hereditary, among those of the south, in the family of Cangapol; who leads the Tehuelhets, Chechehets, Huilliches, Pehuenches, and Diuihets, when they join their forces together. They generally encamp at about thirty or forty leagues distance from the enemies country, that they may not be discovered, and send out scouts, to examine the places they intend to attack; who hide them-

selves

felves during the day, but at night iffue forth from their lurking places, and mark, with the greateft exactnefs, every houfe and farm of the ftraggling villages they intend to attack, fo as to give an account of their difpofition, the number of their inhabitants, and their means of defence. When they have thus informed themfelves, they communicate the intelligence to the main army, who take the time when the moon is paft the full, that they may have light for their work, to march to the affault. When they approach the place, they feparate in fmall bodies, each of which is appointed to attack fome houfe or farm. A few hours after midnight they make the affault, kill all the men who refift, and carry away the women and children for flaves. The Indian women follow their hufbands, armed with clubs, bowls, and fometimes fwords; and ravage and plunder the houfes of every thing they can find, that may be of fervice to them, as cloaths, houfhold utenfils, &c. Thus loaded with booty, they retire as faft as they can; refting neither day nor night, till they are at a great diftance, and out of danger of being overtaken by their enemies; which is fometimes a hundred leagues from the place of the attack. Here they ftop, and divide their booty; which is feldom accomplifhed without great difcontents from fome or other of them, and thefe often terminate in quarrels and bloodfhed.

At other times, they make a kind of flying war, with fmall camps, of fifty or a hundred men in each In this cafe they do not attack whole villages, but only fingle farms or houfes, which they do very haftily, and retire as foon as they can.

The Caciques neverthelefs have not the power to raife taxes, nor to take away any thing from their vaffals; nor can they oblige them to ferve in the leaft employment, without

paying

paying them. On the contrary, they are obliged to treat their vaffals with great humanity and mildnefs, and oftentimes to relieve their wants, or they will feek the protection of fome other Cacique. For this reafon, many of the Elmens, or thofe who are born Caciques, refufe to have any vaffals; as they coft them dear, and yield but little profit. No Indian, or body of Indians, can live without the protection of fome Cacique, according to their law of nations; and if any of them attempted to do it, they would undoubtedly be killed, or carried away as flaves, as foon as they were difcovered.

In cafe of any injury, notwithftanding the authority of the Cacique, the party aggrieved often endeavours to do himfelf juftice to the beft of his power. They know of no punifhment, or fatisfaction, but that of paying, or redeeming the injury, or damage done, with fomething of value in their eftimation (for they ufe no money) nor do they chaftize, but by death. Yet when the offence is not very great, and the offender is poor, the party injured generally beats him with his ftone bowls, on the back and ribs. When the offender is too powerful, they let him alone; unlefs the Cacique interferes, and obliges him to make fatisfaction.

Their wars, in which the different nations engage one with another, and alfo with the Spaniards, arife fometimes from injuries received, which they are eager to revenge; but often from want of provifions, or a defire of plunder.

Although the different nations are at continual variance among themfelves, yet they often join together againft the Spaniards, and choofe an Apo, or Captain-general, to command the whole: at other times, each nation makes war for itfelf. In the wars with the Spaniards of Buenos-Ayres, the Moluches are as auxiliaries, and the Chiefs are chofen from

among

among the Puelches, becaufe they are better acquainted with that country. For the like reafon, in the wars with the Spaniards of Chili, the Chiefs are elected from among the Caciques of the Moluches.

Their marriages are made by fale; the hufband buying his wife of her neareft relations, and oftentimes at a dear price, of beads, cafcabels, garments, horfes, or any thing elfe that is of value among them. They often agree for their wives, and pay part of the price for them, when they are very young, and many years before they are marriageable. Each Indian may have as many wives as he can buy or keep. Widows and orphans are at their own difpofal, and may accept of whom they pleafe: the reft are obliged to abide by the fale, even againft their inclinations, or they are dragged away and compelled to fubmit. It feldom happens that any Indian has more than one wife; though fome have had two or three at a time; efpecially the Elmens, Yas, or Caciques. The reafon of this is, that they are not over-ftocked with women; and thofe which they have are fo dear, that many have no wife at all.

They ufe little or no ceremony in their marriages. At the time agreed upon, the parents lead the lady to the fpoufe's habitation, and deliver her up to him; or he goes and takes her away from her parents, as his own property; and fome-times fhe even goes of herfelf, being certain of a good re-ception. The following morning fhe is vifited by her rela-tions, before the time of rifing; and being found in bed with her fpoufe, the marriage is concluded. But as many of thefe marriages are compulfive on the fide of the woman, they are frequently fruftrated. The contumacy of the woman fome-times tires out the patience of the man, who then turns her away, or fells her to the perfon on whom fhe has fixed her

affections;

affections; but feldom beats her, or treats her ill. At other times the wife elopes from her hufband, and goes to a gallant; who, if he is more powerful, or of a higher rank than the hufband, obliges him to put up with the affront, and to acquiefce in the lofs of his wife; unlefs a more powerful friend obliges the gallant to a reftitution, or to compound the matter; and in thefe affairs they are generally very eafy.

The women, who have once accepted their hufbands, are in general very faithful and laborious. Indeed their lives are but one continued fcene of labour; for, befides the nurfing and bringing up their children, they are obliged to fubmit to every fpecies of drudgery. In fhort they do every thing, except hunting and fighting; and fometimes they even engage in the latter. The care of all houfhold affairs is left entirely to the women: they fetch wood and water, drefs victuals, make, mend, and clean the tents, drefs and few together the hides, and alfo the leffer fkins of which they make their mantles or carapas, and fpin and make ponchas or macuns. When they travel, the women pack up every thing, even the tent-poles; which they muft erect and pull down themfelves, as often as occafion requires: they load, unload, and fettle the baggage, ftraiten the girths of the faddles, and carry the lance before their hufbands. No excufe of ficknefs, or being big with child, will relieve them from the appointed labour: and fo rigidly are they obliged to perform their duty, that their hufbands cannot help them on any occafion, or in the greateft diftrefs, without incurring the higheft ignominy. The women of quality, or thofe related to the Caciques, are permitted to have flaves, who eafe their miftreffes of the moft laborious part of their work; but if they fhould not have any flaves, they muft undergo the fame fatigue as the reft.

It

It is the province of the hufband to provide food; which is generally the flefh of horfes, oftriches, guanacoes, hares, wild-boars, armadilloes, antas, &c. or whatever the country produces. He alfo fupplies his wife with fkins for the tent, and for cloathing; though they often purchafe for them cloaths or mantles of European goods, of the Spaniards; and alfo brafs-earings, cafcabels, and large glafs beads of a fky-blue colour, for which they have a great preference. I have feen them exchange a poncha, or mantle, of their little foxes fkins, which are as fine and as beautiful as ermine, worth from five to feven dollars each, for four ftrings of thefe beads, which are worth about fourpence. The Moluches maintain fome flocks of fheep for their wool, and fow a fmall quantity of corn: but the Puelches depend entirely on their hunting; for which purpofe they keep great numbers of dogs, which they call tehua.

Although their marriages are at will, yet when once the parties are agreed, and have children, they feldom forfake each other, even in extreme old-age. The hufband protects his wife from all injuries, and always takes her part, even if fhe is in the wrong; which occafions frequent quarrels and bloodfhed: but this partiality does not prevent him from reprimanding her in private, for engaging him in thefe difputes. He feldom beats her; and if he catches her in any criminal commerce, lays all the blame on the gallant; whom he corrects with great feverity, unlefs he atones for the injury by fome valuable prefent. They have fo little decency in this refpect, that oftentimes, at the command of the wizards, they fuperftitioufly fend their wives to the woods, to proftitute themfelves to the firft perfon they meet. Yet there are fome women whofe modefty gets the better of their obedience, and who

who refufe to fulfil the defires both of their hufbands and the wizards.

They breed up their children in a vicious indulgence of their humours. The Tehuelhets, or Southern Patagonians, carry this folly to the greateft excefs; and the old people are led about from one place to another, frequently changing their habitations, to humour the caprices of their children. The following account may give an idea, to what a degree of folly they carry this fondnefs. If an Indian, even a Caci-que, refolve to change his habitation, with his family, &c. and is at that time an inhabitant among a different tribe of people, who do not choofe to part with him, it is the cuftom to take one of his children, and to pretend fuch a fondnefs for it, that they cannot part with it; and by thefe means the father is fatisfied, and agrees to ftay: they then deliver him his child, and, inftead of refenting their conduct, he is greatly pleafed that his child is fo much beloved.

The widow of a Tehuel Cacique, whofe hufband had been treacheroufly killed by the Spaniards in time of peace, was determined to leave the town and the miffionaries, and no entreaties or perfuafions were able to quiet her on fo fad an occafion. She had a fon about fix years of age, who was very fond of the miffionaries, on account of the prefents of bread, figs, raifins, &c. which they ufed to give him; and when he underftood that his mother was preparing to carry him away, he would not fuffer himfelf to be dreffed for the journey, and defired to be carried to the fathers. The mo-ther, moved with the diftrefs of her child, confented to remain where fhe was, and foon afterwards became a Chriftian.

The drefs of thefe Indians is very remarkable. The men wear no caps upon their heads, but have their hair tied up behind, with the points upwards; binding it many times above the head with a large girdle of dyed woollen ftuff, curioufly wrought. In their tents they wear a mantle, made of fkins fewed together. Thofe made with the fkins of young colts and mares are the leaft valuable. The mantles made of the fkins of a fmall, ftinking animal, like our pole-cat, which they call yaguane, are fuperior to thefe laft. This animal is of a dark, fable colour, with two large white ftreaks on each fide of it's ribs; it's hair very foft and fine.

The fur of the coipu, or otter, is in equal efteem with that of the yaguane, or maikel. The head, mouth and teeth of this animal very much refemble thofe of a rabbit: it's fur is long and fine, and as good as that of a beaver. It digs it's caves (which confift of one or two ftories) in the banks of rivers, and lives upon fifh. It has a long, round, tapering tail, like that of a rat; and it's flefh is very good to eat.

The mantles made of the fkins of guanacoes are in ftill greater eftimation than thofe before-mentioned, on account of the warmth and finenefs of their wool, and their long duration. But thofe which are in the higheft efteem of all are made with the fkins of fmall foxes, which are exceedingly foft and beautiful. They are of a mottled grey, with a red caft, but not fo durable as thofe of the guanaco.

They alfo make or weave (the Tehuelhets and Chechehets excepted) fine mantles of woollen yarn, beautifully dyed with many colours; which when wrapped round their bodies, reach from their fhoulders to the calf of the leg. They have another, of the fame kind, round the waift, and, befides thefe, a fmall three-cornered leathern apron, that ferves for breeches. They tie two corners of it round their waifts, and pafs the other between their legs, and faften it behind.

behind. They likewife make mantles of red ftuffs, fuch as everlafting, &c. which they buy of the Spaniards; as alfo hats, which they are fond of wearing, efpecially on horfe-back. They adorn themfelves with fky-coloured beads; tying one or two rows of them round their necks and wrifts. They alfo paint their faces, fometimes with red, at other times with black; making themfelves exceedingly ugly and hideous, though they imagine there is great beauty in it.

When they are on horfeback, inftead of the mantle be-fore-mentioned, they ufe one adorned with a greater variety of figures; which has a flit in the middle, through which they put their heads; and the mantle hangs down to their knees, and fometimes to their feet. Both men and women ufe a kind of boots or ftockings, made of the fkin of the thighs and legs of mares and colts; which they firft flay from the fat and inward membranes, and, after drying, foften with greafe; then make them pliant by wringing, and put them on without either fhaping or fewing.

Their defenfive arms confift of a helmet, made like a broad-brimmed hat, of a bull's hide fewed double, and of a coat of mail; which is a wide tunic, fhaped and put on like a fhirt, with narrow fhort fleeves, made of three or four folds of the anta's fkin. It is very heavy, ftrong enough to refift either arrows or lances; and fome fay it is bullet-proof. It is made very high in the neck-part, and almoft covers the eyes and nofe. On foot they ufe likewife a large, un-wieldy, fquare target, of bulls hides. Their offenfive arms are a fhort bow, and arrows pointed with bone. The Te-huelhets and Huilliches fometimes envenom the points, with a fpecies of poifon, which deftroys fo flowly, that the wound-ed perfon lingers for two or three months; till, reduced to a fkeleton, he at laft expires. They likewife ufe a lance, of

L l

four or five yards in length, made of a folid cane, that grows near the Cordillera, with many joints, about four or five inches from one another, and pointed with iron. They have fwords, when they can get them from the Spaniards; but they are in general very fcarce. Another fort of weapons, peculiar to this nation, are bowls, or large, round ftones, fhaped into that form by being beat againft each other, and about four inches in diameter. They are in general pebbles, though I have feen fome, which were brought from within land, that were made of a kind of ore, refembling a fine, light copper. There are others made of a kind of iron-ftone.

These bowls are of two or three forts. That which is moft ufed in war is a fingle, round bowl, of about a pound weight, to which they faften a fmall rope, made of hide or finews. With this they ftrike the adverfary's head, to dafh out his brains; and fometimes throw it, rope and all.

There is another kind, which is indifferently ufed either in war or hunting. This confifts of two bowls, like the former, covered with fkin, and faftened at each end of a long rope of hide, three or four yards in length. They take one of them in their hand, and whirling the other three or four times round their head, throw it, and entangle either man or beaft. They will throw them with fuch dexterity, as to faften a man to his horfe; and will alfo contrive to throw them in fuch a manner, when they are hunting, that the rope fhall twift round the neck of the beaft, and the bowls hang between his legs, fo that he is foon thrown down and taken.

Sometimes, efpecially in hunting, they ufe two leffer bowls, which they faften, with two ropes of about a yard each, to the rope to which the larger ones are tied, that they may entangle their prey the better. In hunting oftriches, deer, or guanacoes, they ufe bowls of a fmaller fize than any

I have

I have yet mentioned. Thefe are made of marble, well po-lifhed, and faftened to a cord made of finews.

The women have no attire for their heads, but have their long hair plaited in two large treffes, which hang down on either fide. They wear ear-rings, or pendants, of fquare brafs plates, about two or three inches broad, and as many deep, with a piece of the fame metal well hammered to pre-vent their ears, which are very widely bored, from being cut. They wear ftrings of fky-blue beads round their necks, arms, and ankles.

They have the fame kind of mantle as the men; but they put one end of it round their necks, faftening it before with a brafs fkewer or pin, and gather it up round the waift; letting it fall down to their ankles. They have alfo a fhort apron, tied about their middle under the mantle, which covers them only before, and reaches a little below the knee. This is woven of dyed yarn, and ftriped from the top to the bottom with different colours. When they ride, they ufe a ftraw hat, of the figure of a broad, low cone; fuch as the Chinefe are reprefented to wear: and their boots are the fame as thofe which are worn by the men.

CHAPTER

CHAPTER VI.

An Account of the Language of the Inhabitants of thefe Countries.

THE languages of thefe Indians differ from each other. I only learned that of the Moluches; it being the moft polifhed, and the moft generally underftood. A confiderable abfence from thefe countries has rendered the recollection very difficult: however, I fhall give the beft account of it I am able, to fatisfy the curious and inquifitive.

This language is much more copious and elegant, than could have been expected from an uncivilized people.

The nouns have only one declination, and are all of the common gender. The dative, accufative, and ablative cafes, have all the fame termination, with their fuffix or poftpofition. There are but two numbers, fingular and plural; the dual being expreffed by placing the word epu (which fignifies two) before the word: but the pronouns have all the three numbers. The adjectives are put before the fubftantives, and do not vary their terminations, either in cafe or number: as,

Cume	*good,*
Cume huentu	*a good man,*
Cume huentu eng'n	*good men.*

The

The Declination of the Nouns.

	Singular.	
N.	Huentu,	*the man,*
G.	Huentuni,	*of the man,* &c.
D.	Huentumo,	
A.	Huentumo,	
V.	Huentu,	
A.	Huentumo,	
	or Huentu engu,	

	Plural.	
N.	Pu huentu or } *the men.*
	huentu eng'n }
G.	Pu huentu, *of the men.*
	and fo on, as in the fingular.

The Pronouns.

Inche,	I,
Eimi,	*thou,*
Vei,	*he,*
T'va or T'vachi,	*this,*
Velli,	*that,*
Inei,	*whom,*

Quifu,	{ *he alone or himfelf*
Inche quifu,	*I myfelf,*
Inchiu,	*we two,*
Inchin,	*we many.*

And in the fame manner,

Eimi,	*thou,*	Eim'n	*you many.*
Eimu,	*you two,*		

For pronouns poffeffive is ufed the genitive, or fign of the genitive, of the pronouns; ni, mine; mi, thine. Likewife m'ten, only; ufed fometimes as an adjective or pronoun, and at other times as an adverb.

The verbs have only one conjugation, and are never irregular or defective. They are formed from any part of fpeech, either by giving it the termination of a verb, or adding to it the verb fubftantive gen, or, as it is pronounced, 'ngen, which anfwers to the Latin verb fum, es, fui, &c.

M m   EXAMPLES.

E X A M P L E S.

1. P'lle,   *near,*
   P'llen *or* P'llengen,   *I am near,*
   P'lley *or* P'llengey,   *he is near.*

2. Cume,   *good,*
   Cumen,
   Cumengen,   } *to be good.*
   Cumelen,

3. Ata,   *Evil* or *bad,*
   Atan,
   Atangen,   } *to be bad,*
   Atal'n *or* Atalcan,   *to corrupt* or *make bad.*

The verbs have three numbers, fingular, dual, and plural; and as many tenfes as in the Greek tongue; all of which they form by interpofing certain particles before the laft letter of the indicative, and before the laft fyllable of the fubjunctive: as,

Prefent tenfe,	Elun,	*to give.*
Imperfect,	Elubun,	
Perfect,	Eluyeen,	
Preterperfect,	Eluyeebun,	
Firft Aorift,	Eluabun,	
Second Aorift,	Eluyeabun,	
Firft Future,	Eluan,	
Second Future,	Eluyean.	

In the fubjunctive mood they terminate with the particle li, ftriking off the letter n in the indicative, and varying all the tenfes as before: as,

Prefent

Prefent tenfe,	Eluli,
Imperfect,	Elubuli,
Perfect,	Eluyeeli,
Preterperfect,	Eluyeebuli.
Firft Aorift,	Eluabuli,
Second Aorift,	Eluyeabuli,
Firft Future,	Eluali,
Second Future,	Eluyeali.

N. B. The Huilliches frequently ufe, inftead of eluyeen, in the perfect tenfe of the indicative, or eluyeeli, in that of the fubjunctive, eluvin and eluvili.

I remarked that, for the imperative, they frequently ufed the future of the indicative, and fometimes in the third perfon; as, Elupe, *Let him give.*

A Moluche Indian, eating an oftrich's egg, and wanting falt, I heard him fay, " Chafimota iloavinquin," *Let me eat it with falt.* Now iloavin is the firft future, with the particle vi interpofed, to fignify *it.* I do not know whether quin is anything more than a particle of ornament; as in the word chafimota; where the concluding fyllable ta is ufelefs but for the fake of the found; as chafimo, without any addition, is the ablative cafe of chafi, *falt.*

The tenfes are conjugated, through all their numbers, with thefe terminations in the indicative prefent;

Sing.	n	imi	y
Dual	iu	imu	ingu
Plural	in	im'n	ing'n

E X A M P L E.

Sing.	Elun	Eluimi	Eluy
Dual	Eluiu	Eluimu	Eluingu
Plural	Eluin	Eluim'n	Eluing'n.

In the SUBJUNCTIVE.

Sing.	li	limi	liy.
Dual	liu	limu	lingu.
Plural	liin	lim'n	ling'n.

EXAMPLE.

Sing.	Eluli	Elulimi	Eluliy.
Dual	Eluliu	Elulimu	Elulingu.
Plural	Eluliin	Elulim'n	Eluling'n.

In this manner all the other tenfes are conjugated.

N. B. The Second Aorift and the Second Future are only ufed by the Picunches, and not by the Huilliches.

The infinitive mood is formed of the firft perfon of the indicative, with the genitive of the primitive pronoun put before, or a poffeffive pronoun, to fignify the perfon that acts or fuffers, and may be taken from any of the tenfes: as,

Ni elun,	*I to give,*
Ni Elubun,	*thou to give,*
Ni Eluvin, &c.	*he to give.*

The other poffeffives are mi, thine; and 'n, his; for thefe are only ufed in the fingular.

There are two participles, formed in the fame manner as the infinitive, to be conjugated through all the tenfes; the one active, the other paffive:

Active,	Elulu,	*the perfon giving.*
Paffive,	Eluel,	*the thing given.*

From

From thefe are derived,

Elubulu,	*he that did give,*
Eluyelu,	*he that has given,*
Elualu,	*he that will give,*
Eluabulu,	*he that was to give,*
Elubuel,	*the thing that was given,*
Eluyeel,	*the thing that has been given,*
Elual, &c.	*the thing that will be given.*

Of all thefe, and of the active verbs, paffives are formed, by adding the verb fubftantive, gen; in which cafe, in all the tenfes, the variation or declenfion changes the verb fubftantive, the adjective verb remaining invariable.

E X A M P L E.

Elugen,	*I have given,*
Elugebun,	*I was given,*
Elugeli,	*I can be given,*
Elungeuyeeli,	*I may have been given,*
Elungeali, &c.	*I fhall have been given.*

Another accident, which the verbs in this language fuffer, is that of tranfition: whereby they fignify, as well the perfon that acts, as him on whom the action paffes, by the interpofition or addition of certain determinate particles to exprefs it. This is common to them with thofe of Peru; but the latter ufe thofe which are more difficult, and in a greater number. I do not think that the languages of the nations of the Puelches, of the Chaco, or the Guaranies, have this particular property. I do not believe I can recollect them all; but I fhall endeavour to give the beft account I can of thefe tranfitions.

The

The tranfitions are fix in number·
From *me* to *thee* or *you*,
From *you* to *me*,
From *him* to *me*,
From *him* to *you*,
From *me* or *you* to *him*,

And the mutual, when it is reciprocal on both fides.

The firft tranfition is expreffed by eymi, eymu, and eim'n, in the indicative; and elmi, elmu, and elm'n, in the fubjunctive; and this runs through all the tenfes: as,

Elun,	*I give*,
Elueymi,	*I give to you*,
Elueymu,	*I give to you two*,
Elueim'n,	*I or we give to you many*.

And in the fubjunctive,
Eluelmi,
Eluelmu,
Eluelm'n,

With their derivatives, the other tenfes.

The fecond tranfition is from *you* to *me*, and is expreffed by the particle en; as eluen, *you give to me*; which has elueiu and eluein, dual and plural.

The third tranfition from *him* to *me*, is

Sing.	Elumon,
Dual	Elumoiu,
Plural	Elumoin (*when we are many.*)

In the fubjunctive it is,

Sing.	Elumoli,
Dual	Elumoliyu,
Plural	Elumoliin.

The

The fourth tranſition, from *him* to *thee*, is formed by adding eneu to the firſt perſon ſingular; as,

Elueneu, he gives to thee;

And eymu mo, eim'n mo, to the dual and plural;

And in the ſubjunctive,

Elmi mo,
Elmu mo,
Elm'n mo.

The fifth tranſition, from *me* to *thee*, to *this*, or *that*, or *him*, is formed by the interpoſition of the particle vi; as,

Eluvin,	*I give it, or give him,*
Eluvimi,	*thou giveſt him,*
Eluvi,	*he giveth him,*
Eluviyu, }	*we or you two give to*
Eluvimu, }	*him, or give it.*
Eluviu, }	
Eluvim'n, }	*we many give to him, or give it.*

The ſubjunctive is Eluvili.

This I perceive to be ſomething equivocal with the perfect tenſe of the Huilliches: yet they like to uſe it, though they themſelves know the impropriety of it. Nor is this the only ground of equivocation in their tongue, which is found eſpecially in the prepoſitions; where one having many ſignifications, the meaning is oftentimes very much confuſed; as may be ſeen in the declination of their nouns.

The ſixth and laſt tranſition is conjugated through all the numbers, moods, and tenſes, in the ſame manner as the ſimple verbs, and is formed by the interpoſition of the particle huu, or, as it is pronounced, wu; as,

Eluhuun,

Eluhuun, *or* } *I give to myfelf,*
Euwun,

Ayuwimi, *thou lovefl thyfelf,*

Ayuhui, *he loveth himfelf,*

Ayuhuim'n, &c. *you love one another.*

They have another particular mode of compounding verbs, altering their fignifications, making affirmatives negatives, neuters actives, and of fignifying and expreffing how and in what manner the thing is done, by the interpofition of prepofitions, adverbs, adjectives, &c. as,

Cupan, *to come,*

Naucupan, *to come downwards.*

Nag'n, *to fall,*

Nagcumen, *to make to fall.*

Payllac'non, *to put one's mouth upwards;*

from pailla, *mouth upwards,* and c'non, *to put.*

Aucan, *to rebel,*

Aucatun, *to rebel over again,*

Aucatul'n, *to make to rebel.*

Lan, *death* or *to die,*

Langm'n, *to kill,*

Langm'chen, *to kill Indians;*

from langm'n, *to kill,* and che, *Indian* or *man.*

Ayun, *to love,*

Ayulan, *not to love.*

Pen fignifies *to fee;* pevin is *I faw him;* vemge, *on this manner;* and la is the negative. Thefe words are compounded into one, thus, pevemgelavin, *I faw him not on this manner.*

The

The numeral words in this language are compleat, and may be ufed to defcribe any number whatfoever.

Quine,	*one,*	Meli,	*four,*	Cayu,	*fix,*
Epu,	*two,*	Kechu,	*five,*	Selge,	*feven,*
Quila,	*three,*				

Mari (*or* Maffi as the Huilliches have it)   *ten,*

Pataca, *a hundred,*   Huaranca, *a thoufand.*

The intermediate numbers are compofed as follows;

Maffi quine,	*eleven,*	Epu maffi epu,	*twenty two,*
Maffi epu,	*twelve,*	Epu maffi quila,	*twenty three,*
Maffi quila,	*thirteen,*	Quila pataca,	*three hundred*
Epu maffi,	*twenty,*	Selge pataca,	*feven hundred.*

The   A D V E R B S, *&c.*

Mu,	*no,*
May,	*yes,*
Chay *or* Chayula,	*to-day,* or *prefently*
Vule,	*to-morrow,*
T'vou,	*here,*
Vellu,	*there,*
P'lle,	*near,*
Allu mapu,	*afar off,*
Nau,	*under,* or *downwards,*
Huenu,	*above,*
Pule,	*againfl,*
Allu pule,	*diftant,*
Chumgechi,	*on what manner,*
Vemgechi *or* vemge,	*on this manner,*
Mo, *or* meu,	{ the Latin prepofitions, *in,* *contra, cum, per, ob, propter,* *intra,*

Cay, and Chay, placed after a noun, *or, alone, and, perhaps,*

Huecu,   *without.*

To

To give some further idea of this language, I add the following specimens of it.

The SIGN of the CROSS.

Santa cruz ni gnelmeu, inchin in pu
By the sign of the holy cross, from our
caynemo montulmoin, Dios, inchin in
enemies deliver us, O GOD, *our*
Apo; Chao, Votch'm cay, Spiritu Santo cay,
Lord; the Father, and Son, and the Holy Ghost,
ni wimeu. Amen.
in the name of. Amen.

The Beginning of the LORD's PRAYER.

Inchin in Chao, huenumeuta m'leymi,
Our Father, in Heaven thou that art,
ufchingepe mi wi; eymi mi toquin
hallowed be thy name; thy kingdom
inchinmo cupape; eymi mi piel,
to us may it come; thy will,
chumgechi vemgey huenu-mapumo,
as it is done in Heaven,
vemgechi cay vemengepe tue-mapumo; &c.
so likewise may it be done on earth; &c.

The Beginning of the CREED.

Mupiltun Dios, Chaomo vilpepilvoe, huenu
I believe in GOD, *the Father Almighty, of Heaven*
vemvoe, tue vemvoe cay; inchin in Apo
the maker, and of earth the maker also; in our Lord
Jefu Chriftomo cay, veyni m'ten Votch'm, &c.
JESUS CHRIST *also, his only Son, &c.*

The

The Beginning of the Chriſtian Doctrine.

Q. Chumten Dios m'ley?   *How many Gods are there?*
A. Quine m'ten.   *One only.*

Q. Cheu m'ley ta Dios?   *Where is* GOD?
A. Huenu-mapumo, tue-mapumo,   *In Heaven, in earth,*
vill-mapumo ſume cay,   *and in all the world whereſoever.*

Q. Iney cam Dios?   *Who is* GOD?
A. Dios Chao, GOD *the Father,* Dios Votch'm, GOD *the Son,*
Dios Spiritu Santo;   cay quila Perſona geyum,
GOD *the Holy Ghoſt;   and being three Perſons,*
quiney Dios m'ten, *are one* GOD *only.*

Q. Chumgechi, quila Perſona geyum,   quine m'ten ta Dios?
*How, being three Perſons,   * GOD *is one alone?*
A. T'vachi quila Perſona quine
Theſe three Perſons have one only
gen-n'gen, veyula quine m'ten ta Dios.
Being, for this GOD *is one alone.*

Theſe ſpecimens are accommodated to the Indian ex-
preſſion, and intermixed with a few Spaniſh words, where
the Indian idiom is inſufficient, or might give a falſe idea.
And this, with the ſhort vocabulary annexed, may ſuffice to
give a ſmall but imperfect notion of this language.

I omit ſeveral common words, becauſe they have been
already explained.

VOCABULARY.

P'LLU, the foul, a fpirit.
Lonco, the head, the hair.
Az, the face.
N'ge, the eyes.
Wun or Huun, the mouth.
Gehuun, the tongue.
Yu, the nofe.
Vofo, the teeth, the bones.
Anca, the body.
Pue, the belly.
Cuugh, the hand.
Namon, the foot.
Pinque, the heart.
P'nen, a child.
Nahue, a daughter.
Peni, a brother.
Penihuen, own brothers.
Huinca, a Spaniard.
Seche, a neat Indian.
Huenuy, a friend.
Caynie, an enemy.
Huincha, a head-fillet.
Makun, a mantle.
Lancattu, glafs-beads;
Cofque, bread.
Ipe, food.
In, or ipen, to eat.
Ilo, flefh.
Ilon, to eat flefh.
Putun, drink, to drink.
Putumum, a cup.
Chilca, writing.
Chilcan, to write.
Sengu, a word, language; alfo a thing.
Huayqui, a lance.
Huayquitun, to lance.
Chinu, a knife, a fword.
Chingofcun, to wound.
Chingofquen, to be wounded.
Conan, a foldier.
Conangean, he that is to be a foldier.
Amon, to walk or go.
Anun, to fit.
Anupeum, a feat or ftool.

Anunmahuun, to feel inwardly.
Poyquelhuun, to feel, or perceive.
Con'n, to enter.
Tipan, to go out.
Cupaln, to bring.
Entun, to take away.
Afeln, to be averfe.
Afelgen, to hate.
M'len, to be, to poffefs.
Mongen, life, to live.
Mongetun, to revive.
Suam, the will.
Suamtun, to will.
Pepi, power.
Pepilan, to be able.
Quimn, knowledge, to know.
Quimeln, to learn.
Quimelcan, to teach.
Pangi, a lion.
Choique, an oftrich.
Achahual, a cock or hen.
Malu, a large lizard or iguana.
Cufa, a ftone, an egg.
Saiguen, a flower.
Milya, gold.
Lien, filver.
Cullyin, money, payment.
Cullingen, to be rich.
Cunnubal, poor, miferable, an orphan.
Cum panilhue (red metal) copper.
Chos panilhue (yellow metal) brafs,
Gepun, colour, or painting.
Saman, a trade, an artificer.
Mamel, a tree, wood.
Mamel-faman, a carpenter.
Suca-faman, a houfe-builder.
Antuigh, the fun, a day.
Cuyem or Kiyem, the moon, a month.
Tipantu, a year.
K'tal, fire.
Afee, hot.
Chofee, cold.
Atutuy, it is fhivering cold.

THE END.

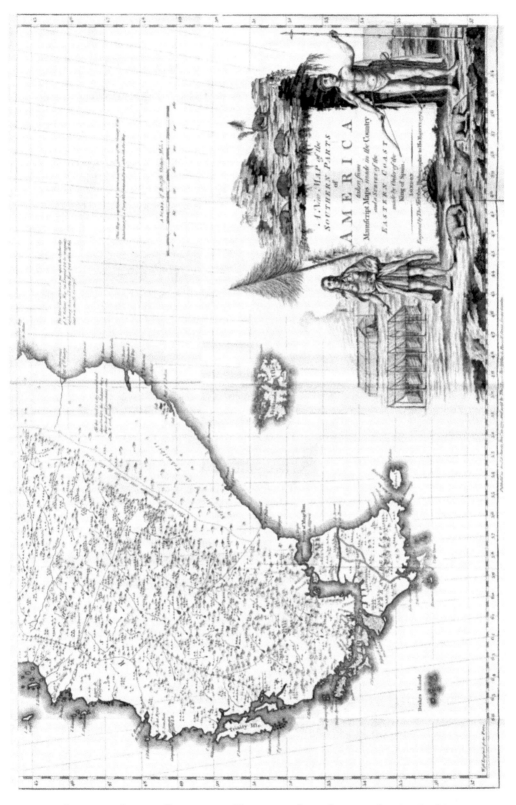

The material originally positioned here is too large for reproduction in this reissue. A PDF can be downloaded from the web address given on page iv of this book, by clicking on 'Resources Available'.

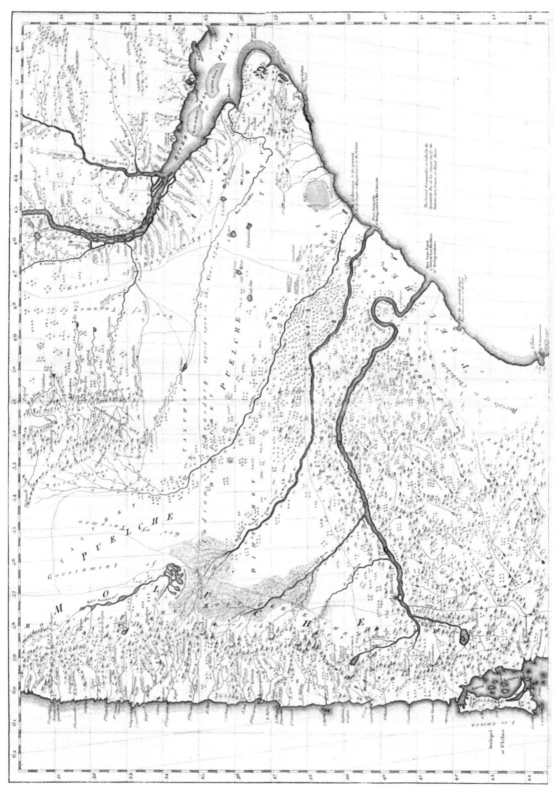

The material originally positioned here is too large for reproduction in this reissue. A PDF can be downloaded from the web address given on page iv of this book, by clicking on 'Resources Available'.